Have you ever wondered why some ideas just never seem to go away, even though they keep causing problems? Think about it: there are certain ideas that, no matter how much damage they do, still manage to stick around. They're like a nasty insect that just won't die, no matter how much you try to kill it.

We're talking about things like taxes that take away your hard-earned money, government schools that fail to teach you what really matters, bureaucracies that slow everything down, and gun control laws that leave good people defenseless. These are the ideas that keep getting recycled and pushed on us, despite all the evidence that they don't work—or worse, that they actually cause harm.

But why do these ideas persist?

Why do people keep supporting things like the minimum wage when it just ends up hurting the very people it's supposed to help? Why do governments spy on their citizens in the name of security, even though it invades our privacy and freedom? These are the world's worst ideas, and yet, they keep coming back, generation after generation.

The List of the
WORST IDEAS

THE TUTTLE TWINS GUIDE TO
THE WORLD'S WORST IDEAS

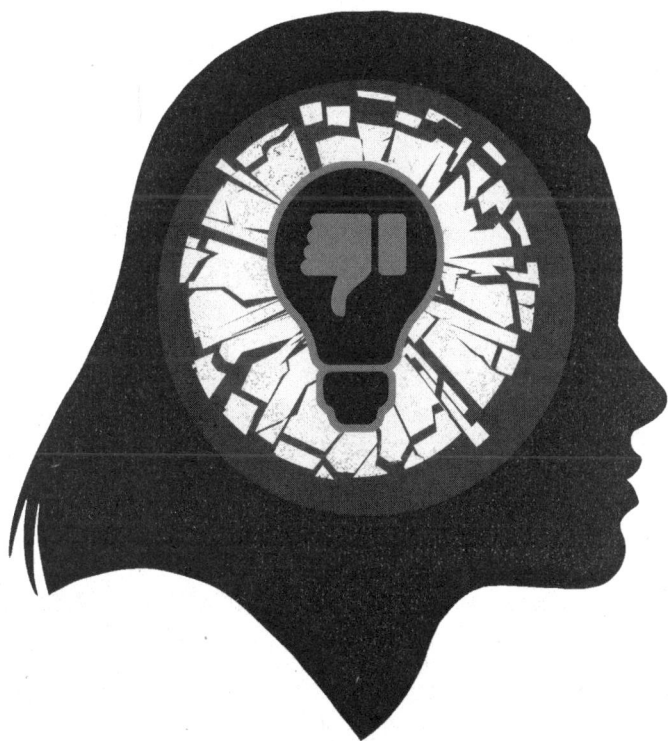

BY CONNOR BOYACK

ISBN 979-8-88688-032-8

Boyack, Connor, author.
Stanfield, Cathryn Shahan, illustrator.
The Tuttle Twins Guide to the World's Worst Ideas / Connor Boyack.

Cover design by Elijah Stanfield
Edited and typeset by Connor Boyack

Printed in Canada

10 9 8 7 6 5 4 3 2 1

It's easy to get frustrated, but here's the thing: understanding why these bad ideas are so popular is the first step to fighting back against them.

That's why we've put together this guide. Each chapter will dive into one of these terrible ideas, showing you not only how they harm society but also why people continue to believe in them.

We're going to break down the myths, expose the truth, and equip you with the knowledge you need to challenge these ideas when you encounter them. Because here's the reality: these ideas affect all of us now and limit our future potential. It's time to arm yourself with the facts, question the status quo, and stand up against the world's worst ideas.

Are you ready to take on the challenge? Let's get started!

—The Tuttle Twins

GOVERNMENT WELFARE

Government welfare programs often lead to long-term dependency, rather than helping individuals achieve self-sufficiency.

"I think the best way of doing good to the poor is not making them easy in poverty, but leading them out of it. I observed that the more public provisions were made, the less they provided for themselves, and of course became poorer."

~ Benjamin Franklin

Barbara Ehrenreich bounced around between Florida, Maine, and Minnesota, seeking whatever low-skill jobs she could find—living on the edge of poverty. She worked as a waitress, a hotel maid, a cleaning woman, a nursing home aide, and a Wal-Mart sales clerk. Her home was typically in a trailer park, or sometimes a decrepit residential motel.

Ehrenreich was a divorced homemaker reentering the workforce, trying to work her hardest to get ahead and pay her bills. And in 1998, when her employment search started, the going pay for entry-level work was around $7 per hour. With such a low salary, she could only afford around $500 per month for rent—and in Key West, Florida, where she first found a job as a waitress at a dingy restaurant attached to a discount motel, which meant she could only afford a trailer home. The one she found had no air conditioning, no screens, no fans, and no television. In other words, it was effectively a place to sleep and a place where, at every other hour of the day, you would want to be anywhere else.

She wasn't alone in this financial struggle; her new co-workers shared with her how they had been getting by. Annette, a twenty-year-old pregnant server at the restaurant, lived with her mother, who was a postal clerk in town. Marianne, the breakfast server, lived with her boyfriend and paid $680 a month for a one-person trailer. Andy, a cook, lived on a dry-docked boat. Tina, another server, lived with her husband at a local motel, paying $60 per night. Joan, the hostess, lived in her van, parking in a vacant lot behind a nearby shopping center. In short, everyone working for low wages was barely getting by, if you can even call it that. In her own words, here's how Ehrenreich later described it:

There are no secret economies that nourish the poor; on the contrary, there are a host of special costs. If you can't put up the two months' rent you need to secure an apartment, you end up paying through the nose for a room by the week. If you have only a room, with a hot plate at best, you can't save by cooking up huge lentil stews that can be frozen for the week ahead. You eat fast food or the hot dogs and Styrofoam cups of soup that can be microwaved in a convenience store. If you have no money for health insurance… you go without routine care or prescription drugs and end up paying the price…

As the tourist business slows in the summer heat, I sometimes leave work with only $20 in tips (the gross is higher, but servers share about 15 percent of their tips with the busboys and bartenders). With wages included, this amounts to about the minimum wage of $5.15 an hour. The sum in the drawer is piling up but at the present rate of accumulation will be more than $100 short of my rent when the end of the month comes around. Nor can I see any expenses to cut.

It was a tough life. But the toughness was only temporary. Why? Because Barbara Ehrenreich wasn't really poor; this was a social experiment she set up to live on minimum wage and experience poverty to write about it for her 2001 book, *Nickel and Dimed: On (Not) Getting By in America*. Hers was a quest to showcase to the public what life was like on the bottom rungs of society's ladder, and that meant taking mundane, minimum wage jobs and trying to subsist only on her meager wages. "I grew up hearing over and over, to the point of tedium, that 'hard work' was the secret of success," she wrote. "No one ever said that you could work hard—harder even than you ever thought possible—and still find yourself sinking ever deeper into poverty and debt." Her provocative book highlights precisely why government welfare programs were created: to render aid to those in need, of whom there are *many*.

The Context

All humans deserve dignity, of course—and, consequently, everyone should have access to the essentials of life: food and water, shelter, health care, and so on. That's how the conventional argument goes, anyway—the idea that government exists to provide a minimum standard of support for its citizens to ensure that nobody is dying in the street from starvation. So when the Great Depression began with the stock market crash of 1929, with millions of Americans losing their jobs, homes, and life savings overnight, what was the appropriate response by the government?

In the wake of this economic turmoil, President Franklin D. Roosevelt introduced the New Deal, a series of programs, public work projects, financial reforms, and regulations. Among these were key welfare initiatives like the Social Security Act, which provided unemployment insurance and aid to the disabled, elderly, and families with dependent children. This marked the beginning of the federal government's role in economic security and welfare—a concerted effort to combat the rampant poverty that characterized the 1930s. And, as significant as these reforms were, they were just the beginning of a broader expansion of welfare programs, particularly during the 1960s.

President Lyndon B. Johnson declared a "War on Poverty" in 1964 as part of his Great Society vision. This initiative aimed to eliminate poverty by improving living conditions and providing more extensive support to the poor. Johnson's administration introduced a variety of programs aimed at reducing poverty's hold on American families, including Medicare and Medicaid, the Food Stamp Act of 1964, and the Economic Opportunity Act. "Our aim is not only to relieve the symptom of poverty," Johnson said, announcing the new initiatives, "but to cure it and, above all, to prevent it." He continued: "We shall not rest until that war is won. The richest nation on Earth can afford to win it. We cannot afford to lose it."

Since human needs are nearly endless, there soon became a welfare program for all sorts of distress: old age, unemployment, illness, poverty, physical disability, loss of spousal support, childrearing needs, workplace injury, consumer misfortune, traffic accident, environmental hazard, and loss from flood, fire, or hurricane. The federal government funds over 100 separate anti-poverty initiatives; add on to this all the state and local programs that exist, and you find a patchwork of programs designed to render aid to those who need it. And proponents of the welfare state—a term that refers to all of these programs put together—believe that more still needs to be done. Clearly, poverty still exists—so more funding and more government initiatives are needed, we're told, in order to better address the problem.

Sure, Ehrenreich's experience was artificial—but the many stories she shared in her book of people subsisting on low income are real. In America and around the world, impoverished individuals worry about their next meal. They don't have the luxury of saving for retirement or going to the movies. They don't have Amazon Prime or a gym membership. It is for these people that such programs are created—the intended beneficiaries of the government largesse that Johnson stated the richest nation can afford. And in this noble effort of helping the poor—one that most religious people consider a commandment, mind you—well-intentioned politicians and bureaucrats have long dangled welfare checks in front of eager voters looking for a handout and a leg up.

The problem? Like the road to hell, the welfare state is paved with good intentions—and neither place is somewhere you want to be.

Why is it the Worst Idea?

First things first. That "War on Poverty" Johnson declared? It was a total disaster—an utter failure. Even six months into the launch of these new programs, a congressional hearing found that things were not going well. And six decades later, the results are clear: over $25 trillion in taxpayer dollars have been wasted on a broken, bureaucratic system that has not stopped poverty. More than a third of Americans receive some type of welfare support—and if you add up all that money, it's five times more than what's needed to eliminate poverty. The bucket of aid intended for the poor is full of holes.

You might be tempted to think that the problem is money management. All that waste! Why, if only we could eliminate the bureaucrats and provide the money directly to the poor people, then we'd solve poverty once and for all, right? Wrong. Simply giving people money does not restore their dignity, nor does it necessarily help them stand up on their own two feet. Instead, it often traps people in a state of dependence, relying on others perpetually. It's a poverty trap—rather than there being a so-called "safety net" to catch people when they stumble and help them quickly recover, it becomes a sticky spider's web that ensnares its prey and prevents escape.

Desiree Metcalf is one of many who fell into the trap and hasn't been able to get out. A twenty-four-year-old mother of three, she lives in a small apartment in western New York.

The Metcalf family has been the beneficiary of a number of welfare programs: food stamps, health care, housing, and Head Start—many of the programs that emerged after Johnson declared war on poverty. But instead of getting a job and becoming self-sufficient, she stays on welfare. The reason, in her own words, is: "If you get a job and they take you off public assistance, then they don't pay for daycare," noting that the cost of child care would consume much of her income. She also noted that if she starts earning money, then she starts losing benefits, like food stamps. The comfort and security of steady welfare checks were too enticing for her; Metcalf was financially disincentivized to get a job.

This isn't what Johnson had in mind at the outset of his war. His stated goal was to make poor families self-sufficient, pulling themselves up and out of poverty through their own earnings without long-term dependence on welfare. But the exact opposite has happened. In the decade prior to the War on Poverty, self-sufficiency in America had been improving significantly, but since that time, there has been no improvement. Many segments of society are less capable of self-support today than they were when Johnson's efforts began.

In addition to trapping people in poverty, government welfare is the worst idea because it undermines the most effective approach to helping the poor: voluntary charity. After all, why would someone donate $100 of their hard-earned money to help the poor if they are already being taxed that much or more for the same purpose? The state's welfare efforts thus disincentivize society to step in and help. And history bears this out completely.

In early America, families, churches, and neighborhoods helped care for the needy, where the common goal was self-reliance. When you know the people helping you—your parents, your friends, your fellow churchgoers—you have a strong motivation to not only stop receiving their aid but also to repay them. This isn't true of a government welfare check, where faceless bureaucrats mail money to your home with no personal connection or pressure to stop the practice. And, in touring early America, Alexis de Tocqueville noted this contrast. Throughout Europe, he observed that the "state almost exclusively undertakes to supply bread to the hungry, assistance and shelter to the sick, work to the idle, and to act as the sole reliever of all kinds of misery." But "in the United States" in the 1800s, he wrote, "you will be sure to find an association." It was extremely common for those in need to form and join fraternal associations that provided health care, life insurance, and other benefits. These voluntary associations of mutual aid were extremely popular among immigrants, minorities, and the working class. Their prime object was "to promote the brotherhood of man… to establish a system for the care of the widows and orphans, the aged and disabled, and enable every worthy member to protect himself from the ills of life." By 1910, their combined membership surpassed 13 million; observers noted that such organizations "honeycombed the slums of Chicago," and among one ethnic minority, the "number of societies passes computation," while the Lower East Side of Manhattan "swarms with voluntary organizations of many kinds."

And beyond formal organizations with their charitable aid, society stepped up in a variety of other ways. One study of 200 wage-earning families in New York City conducted in 1905 revealed that "almost every family of small income received some help or other from friends or relatives in the form of clothing for the children, money for the rent, or occasional gifts to carry the family over a tight place." These informal arrangements dwarfed the efforts of fraternal organizations and represented a *true* social safety net—one whose threads were woven by social institutions, especially the family.

And then the state stepped in. When FDR's New Deal promised support to millions of Americans, the newly created government programs put fraternal societies in full retreat. By assuming the burden of caring for those in need, the government had undermined the very reason these organizations existed. The role of churches shrank dramatically; welfare spending by churches fell 30 percent in response to the New Deal. Voluntary charity, with its focus on self-sufficiency and reciprocity—with recipients of aid finding ways to help out or later paying it forward—quickly gave way to paternalistic dependency. These new welfare programs were justification for the charitable organizations, not only to reject new applicants but to eventually close down entirely. It's hard to solicit donations from people who are already being taxed and told that the government will take care of them in times of need.

This general rule applies whether we're talking about food stamps for families in Savannah, Georgia, or foreign aid to the country of Georgia. When the government hands out monetary assistance using our taxpayer dollars, it severs the connection between payer and recipient. It eliminates the social expectations and pressure that ensure this aid is only temporary. It deprives both parties of a relationship where the giver can render reciprocal support of some kind and show gratitude to the payer. And it ends up creating more of what it aims to combat, which is why the War on Poverty and its related welfare programs have not stopped the condition they sought to stop.

A World Without It

Half a century ago, Bertrand de Jouvenel wrote, "The essential psychological characteristic of our age is the predominance of fear over self-confidence… Everyone of every class tries to rest his individual existence on the bosom of the state and tends to regard the state as the universal provider." But what if, with a hypothetical snap of the fingers, the state ceased to provide? Imagine a world where government welfare programs are phased out and we return the responsibility for social care to individuals and communities. What might that look like?

As stated previously, welfare was already on the decline

prior to launching the War on Poverty. In other words, there is historical evidence for society being self-sustaining without the state; before welfare programs became the norm, people could obtain help from a wide variety of sources. But this dependence was short-lived because people were getting help directly from other humans, often those they knew well. Rather than being disincentivized to work, recipients of voluntary charity were very motivated to not only stop needing support but often to pay it back or pay it forward. They had been the beneficiaries of help, and their hearts had been touched; they were often inspired to want to help others as they had been helped—a reality that strengthened the social fabric and the true social safety net.

But why is it that self-sufficiency was on the rise prior to the War on Poverty? How were poor people rising out of poverty without the government's aid? There are many answers, but one stands out: innovation. Think of this picture: half a billion people in sub-Saharan Africa own cell phones. Most "poor people" in America have a variety of creature comforts. And even Eisenberg's experience, though artificial, revealed how, in many ways, today's poor live better than the kings of old who didn't have refrigerators, microwaves, automobiles, air conditioning, and more. According to the government's own surveys, 80 percent of poor households have air conditioning; nearly two-thirds have cable TV; and half own a personal computer. In fact, 96 percent of poor parents stated that their children were never hungry because they could not afford food. Innovative technologies have created an abundance of items, which has driven down their cost.

The modern economy offers abundance all around us, and innovation is the main driver for lowering costs and making goods and services accessible to the masses. But the conveniences in America in the 2000s might obscure its importance since it's so easy to take for granted what we are all accustomed to. So let's consider something different. Think of a country where fewer than five percent of people have access to electricity and where the average life expectancy is just forty-five years old. Infant mortality is so high that one baby out of every five dies. The average person in this country spends over half of their income on food alone. What impoverished nation would you guess this is? Honduras? Zambia? Burundi?

This country is the United States of America—in the 1800s. In this era, the US was as equally impoverished as today's poorest nations. Infant mortality back then, in the US, was three times higher than it is today in sub-Saharan Africa. Poverty was rampant. What America did have was fertile soil for innovation—a fairly free market economy composed of entrepreneurial individuals looking to build a better future for their families. One such individual was Isaac Merritt Singer, who wanted to empower unskilled workers with a low-cost sewing machine that was accessible to everyone. After much tinkering, he invented a sewing machine that reduced the average time to stitch a shirt from 14 hours to just one! Unskilled workers, using this device, quickly outproduced highly skilled seamstresses, which skyrocketed productivity. In 1858, Singer sold 3,000 of these machines. By 1873, he was selling 7,000 a week. This innovation sparked many others and fueled economic growth in the textile industry. Between 1860 and

1870, the industry doubled and topped a billion dollars by 1890. It offered economic opportunity to the poor while also enabling the production of lower-cost clothing which benefited many poor in need. No government program provided these people with what innovation could and did.

We need not imagine a world without the welfare state, because that world has already existed. Historical evidence makes clear that people can and will step up to help those around them if the state takes a step back. What's imperative is removing the incentives that keep people trapped in welfare programs and restoring the human connection between giver and recipient so as to ensure that welfare support is temporary and limited. Human dignity demands eliminating long-term dependence, and government welfare programs are the worst culprit in perpetuating the problem. As history has shown, when given the freedom to innovate and the responsibility to care for one another, societies thrive—proving that the true path to prosperity lies not in government dependency but in empowering individual initiative and community support.

Tuttle Twins Takeaways

1. Before the introduction of widespread government welfare programs, individuals and communities were often self-reliant, using local resources and mutual aid to support those in need. This included help from family, neighbors, and various community organizations.

2. Historical examples, like the spread of sewing machines in the 1800s, show how innovation has always played a critical role in improving living standards and

providing opportunities for economic advancement, reducing the need for government assistance.

3. Government welfare programs, while typically well-intentioned, can create dependency rather than empowerment, trapping individuals in poverty rather than providing a temporary support system to help them regain their independence.

4. Voluntary charity and mutual aid were historically more effective in fostering a sense of community and personal responsibility. They encouraged recipients to contribute back to society and work toward self-sufficiency—a dynamic that is absent in impersonal government welfare systems.

NEOCON-SERVATISM

A deadly ideology has driven foreign policy toward global intervention, leading to costly wars and entanglements with far-reaching consequences.

"Our military is overextended, our economy is burdened with debt, and our credibility in the world is in question. The neo-conservatives promote endless war, nation-building, and a disregard for the sovereignty of other nations. If we continue down this path, we will find ourselves trapped in perpetual war, with no clear mission and no definable victory."

~ Ron Paul

The Berlin Wall was a concrete barrier that symbolized oppression and division. As it finally crumbled on November 9, 1989, the world watched in awe, shocked that this long-awaited day had finally arrived. In the aftermath of World War II, some 2.5 million residents of East Germany had fled to West Germany in search of a job and a better life. So in 1961, fearing that a continued exodus would destabilize the state and its economy, East Germany erected a barrier built of barbed wire and cinder blocks to trap their citizens and prevent their escape. Later replaced by a series of concrete walls that loomed 15 feet high, the wall was crowned with barbed wire and monitored by guards from watchtowers. There were landmines, electric fences, and a variety of additional fortifications that spanned dozens of miles.

It wasn't just a concrete wall that fell—it was the shattering of an era. President Ronald Reagan had stood near this symbol of division just a couple of years prior, challenging the Soviet leadership with the bold demand: "Mr. Gorbachev, tear down this wall!" His words marked a pivotal moment in the twilight struggle of the Cold War—capping off years of foreign conflict and military tension. And as the wall was torn down by jubilant citizens on both sides, a feeling of euphoria swept over the crowd. One journalist documented several of the responses:

> "I can't believe I'm here," an elderly East Berliner told reporters as he crossed into the West. "This is what we have dreamed of all these years."

> "It's over, it's all over, I can't believe it," said an East German as he ducked to get under the red-and-white

barriers at the Bornholmer Strasse crossing, an act that might have cost him his life several months ago.

"I can't describe it," a young woman said with tears in her eyes. "I would never have believed it possible." A middle-aged East Berliner summed up his feelings with the words: "Joy, entirely great joy."

With good reason, most people were excited for a season of peace in the wake of communism's collapse. An end to war! An opportunity to turn our energies to productive pursuits instead of mutually destructive ones! But peace was not a guarantee, and new conflicts and chaos emerged in the vacuum left by the Soviet Union's collapse. These challenges were seen by some as a call to action—a political faction that called themselves neoconservatives (or "new" conservatives).

The world needed a policeman, this group argued, to guard the fragile order and to ensure that tyranny did not fill the void left by the Soviet Union. And as the neoconservatives obtained positions of power in the government to advance their agenda, they shaped the post-Cold War world, promoting a strong American military involved overseas due to their conviction that freedom needed a protector, and America was fit for the role. The idea of toppling dictators and promoting democracy was not merely an aspect of foreign policy; for neoconservatives, it was a moral imperative. They portrayed America as a proactive force capable of bringing down regimes that threatened their own people and global peace. By framing their actions in moral terms—good versus evil—they connected deeply with American values, especially in times of crisis like the aftermath of September 11. The neoconservative narrative of America being the world's protector had a strong appeal, especially when contrasted with more nuanced or self-centered foreign policy approaches. It catered to the desire for safety and the instinct to defend freedom, wherever it might be threatened.

The operative question we will soon explore is… was an aggressive foreign policy stance like this, casting America as the world's police force, the right call?

The Context

For years, the website banner for *Human Events* boasted that it has been "leading the conservative movement since 1944." Felix Morley was the publication's cofounder and a staunch opponent of foreign intervention. And because of these views, he resigned just six years later, in 1950, over the aggressive military stance that the publisher wished to take toward the Soviet Union. The banner wasn't necessarily wrong; *Human Events* has for years published a chaotic mixture of conservative voices on differing sides of foreign policy, from shrill interventionists to so-called isolationists. But this confusing tension with two totally opposing viewpoints within one "movement"—especially on so important a topic!—pinpoints the problem with conservatism.

On this issue and others, the conservative camp can (and should) be split into differing factions, given their vastly diverging views. Hence, paleoconservative and neoconservative. The prefix *paleo* is Greek, meaning "ancient" or "old." So, those who embrace this term suggest that they are the OG conservatives—an authentic group before those other guys broke off and started spouting nonsense. Those other guys, the neoconservatives (or "neocons" for short), see their paleo counterparts as backwater hillbillies—political ignoramuses who don't realize what's at stake and why America's military presence around the world is so essential.

There are other labels, too—the "Old Right" and its counterpart, the "New Right." The former group was a loose group of academics, politicians, and writers who were opposed to the US getting involved in World War II. And when the Cold War rolled around years later, they continued their opposition in the shadow of the quickly growing New Right—a group of anti-Soviet liberals and social democrats, many of whom preferred to call themselves paleoliberals. (Are you seeing yet how meaningless terms like "left" and "right" can be in trying to describe someone's political worldview?) Whatever the labels used, the point is that neocons are more traditionally leftist in their support of growing the government to accomplish some larger agenda. The fact that most of the newer neocons today were never on the political "left" isn't relevant, as they are the intellectual heirs of older ex-leftists. Neoconservatives aren't actually conservative in the true sense of the word; "conserving" America's long-standing traditions would mean having a humble foreign policy and rejecting the idea of being the world's policeman. After all, in his farewell address in 1796, George Washington warned his successors that America must "steer clear of permanent alliances with any portion of the foreign world."

Yet permanent alliances are what we have today, fueled by the neoconservative narrative. Washington's warning seems almost prophetic when we consider the complex web of military engagements and treaties that the United States has woven since the end of World War II. This web has pulled America into numerous conflicts around the globe, often with the enthusiastic support of neocons who view such entanglements as necessary to maintain global stability and promote democratic values. One of the most significant examples of these permanent alliances is NATO (North Atlantic Treaty Organization). Formed in 1949, NATO was initially intended as a bulwark against Soviet aggression in Europe. But its existence and expansion post-Cold War have only served to commit the US to military actions that have nothing to do with protecting Americans on American soil.

Another example is the numerous defense treaties with countries such as Japan, South Korea, and the Philippines. These treaties not only bind the US to defend these nations in the event of an attack but also maintain a significant American military presence in these regions. This presence is often justified by neocons as a deterrent against potential aggressors like North Korea and China and as a way to support allies in maintaining regional stability. However, these permanent alliances also mean that local conflicts have the potential to quickly escalate into larger international crises involving American soldiers. Or consider the mess that is the Middle East, where neocons agitated to dethrone Saddam Hussein, effect regime change in multiple countries, and fight a "War on Terror." Millions of lives and trillions of taxpayer dollars have been wasted away on this conflict in the Middle East—cheered on loudly by neocons who effectively claim that those who oppose them are weak-kneed, unpatriotic traitors.

From the neoconservative viewpoint, the 9/11 attacks changed everything. Whereas President Bush argued as a candidate on the campaign trail for a restrained foreign policy with no nation-building, his presidency ended up being the exact opposite. In January 2002, he named Iraq, Iran, and North Korea as states that "constitute an axis of evil" that "pose a grave and growing danger." He began advocating for preventive war and meddling in the affairs of other nations: "I will not wait on events, while dangers gather. I will not stand by, as peril draws closer and closer. The United States of America will not permit the world's most dangerous regimes to threaten us with the world's most destructive weapons." It was like Christmas morning for neocons—especially those who had leadership positions in the Bush administration. If they could convince a previously "isolationist" political leader to flip-flop and support their agenda, who couldn't they convince?

Why is it the Worst Idea?

Some questions should easily answer themselves, such as "Why is it bad for the military to be engaged in endless wars that have no connection to national defense?" And yet, many people are swayed by the siren song played by neocons, who use fear and terror to scare people into submission. "Surely we must go fight, for if we do not, then the enemy will eventually find their way to our front door!" So goes the argument. And yet the record is clear: the neoconservative position on foreign policy has resulted in colossal death and destruction and a destabilized world. Millions dead, both soldiers and civilians; countless more displaced from their homes due to destroyed infrastructure and destabilized governments; and trillions of taxpayer dollars spent—both through taxation and inflation, thus worsening the living standard of everyone whose money is now worth less. Every statistic points to the miserable failure of the foreign adventurism espoused by neocons.

And the world isn't safer as a result, as they promised—either abroad or at home. Why at home? Because heavy warfare requires big government; as the saying goes, war is the health of the state. When neoconservative William Buckley, Jr., founded the *National Review* in 1955, he broke from the Old Right over the threat of Cold War communism. He claimed that the stakes were so high that our survival was under siege and that the "invincible aggressiveness" of the Soviet Union required new "battle plans" to fight it. Then he wrote this shocking admission:

> We have got to accept big government for the duration—for neither an offensive nor a defensive war can be waged… except through the instrumentality of a totalitarian bureaucracy within our shores.

Keep in mind that this guy considered himself a conservative—and like most conservatives, he supported enlarging government power to accomplish his desired agenda. Buckley argued that "to beat the Soviet Union, we must, to an extent, imitate the Soviet Union." (To *what* extent?!) Here we see another reason why neoconservatism is a horrible idea—it is a trojan horse masking a massive increase in state power over the individual. And that power doesn't go away once the "emergency" is over. The reason why you still get patted down by the TSA and have the contents of your cell phone exposed to NSA employees and other government goons is because the government does not relinquish its power; once citizens get comfortable with the "new normal," then that becomes the baseline for the state—those in power know that we acclimate quickly to our chains.

Speaking of chains, James Madison was spot on over two centuries ago when he warned that "one legislative interference is but the first link of a long chain of repetitions, every subsequent interference being naturally produced by the effects of the preceding." In simple speak, a government action creates a chain reaction where each action tends to create a situation that justifies another action, and then another, and then another—like a chain that keeps getting longer every time you add a new link. Accepting "big government" and the erosion of our liberty is the legacy of neocons. Not all were willing to publicly admit, like Buckley did, that their views required the growth of the state. But it's the clear reality.

When Dwight D. Eisenhower stepped down as president, he spoke directly to the American people and warned:

> We have been compelled to create a permanent armaments industry of vast proportions… This conjunction of an immense military establishment and a large arms industry is new in the American experience… Yet we must not fail to comprehend its grave implications… In the councils of government, we must guard against the acquisition of unwarranted influence, whether sought or unsought, by the military-industrial complex. The potential for the disastrous rise of misplaced power exists and will persist.

Neocons love the military-industrial complex. They are its lobbyists, its cheerleaders, and its allies. Projecting military strength around the world requires a massive industry of weapons makers and mercenaries. And there are many reasons why this "misplaced power" Eisenhower warned against is so problematic. Here's just one, which many people fail to consider: the research and production of weapons require a significant portion of the scientific and technical workforce. In other words, hundreds of thousands of smart, specialized workers are under the employ of the military-industrial complex. And this reality deprives our society of all kinds of innovations and progress that might be achieved if these individuals instead pursued peacetime pursuits in civilian production. It's a lose-lose proposition; this permanent establishment of military power bleeds taxpayers, wastes scientific knowledge, and harms, kills, and displaces countless individuals. It's a race to the bottom, cheered on by the neocons.

A final note on why their foreign policy views are so awful. Maintaining this level of foreign entanglement requires constantly whipping the public into a frenzy to keep them in fear. If they are scared, they will support fighting the bad guys "over there" so they never come "over here." What this has produced is a ripple effect—or, to use Madison's analogy, a long chain—where the government rules by emergency, using this same tactic. As Rahm Emanuel—Obama's chief of staff—once said, those in power "never let a good crisis go to waste." And if a crisis doesn't exist, you manufacture one. So this rule-by-fear has led to things like the authoritarian response to COVID-19, including shutting down churches, forcing people to self-quarantine, arresting people for going to the beach, and more; bailing out failing banks with taxpayer dollars because of the claim that doing so would spare the economy of even worse outcomes; constant threats of government shutdown because of the debt ceiling; or the passage of the USA PATRIOT Act with its erosion of civil liberties, all in the name of finding and stopping new crises before they emerge. A nation conditioned to surrender its freedom in exchange for security will be repeatedly told of new threats that require "big government for the duration," as Buckley put it. Fool me once, shame on you. Fool me twice, shame on me. It's time we saw through the lies and rejected this evil scheme.

A World Without It

What would a world without neocons look like? It's a provocative question, and nothing less than global security and peace are at stake. This deadly mind virus has swept through society in past decades, infecting its hosts with fear and conditioning them to support aggressive interventions abroad that fuel the growth of the military-industrial complex. But if you could snap your fingers and do away with those who would drag us into more war, what would the world be like?

Let's start with a simple admission: the world would not be rid of evil people. There would still be future dictators and despots oppressing their people in pursuit of power. The history of the world is full of such people, as will be its future. The ultimate question is, what is the better solution:

to invade and intervene in other countries' conflicts or mind our own business?

Minding our own business has the benefit of stopping the cycle of blowback. When a country intervenes militarily in another nation's affairs, it often creates unintended consequences, including fostering resentment and giving rise to new threats. For example, Americans were outraged when some of their fellow citizens were held hostage in Iran in 1979, but few realized at the time that it was retaliation for the CIA's involvement in toppling their elected prime minister, Mohammad Mossadegh, years earlier. Intervention begets retaliation; minding our own business means fewer enemies trying to attack us. If you stick your hand in a hornet's nest, you're just inviting a counterattack.

Minding our own business would also stop the waste of taxpayer dollars and lives, allowing them to be used for productive purposes and economic growth. Trillions of dollars spent on overseas military operations could instead be invested in things that actually benefit taxpayers. The focus would shift from projecting power across the globe to enhancing the quality of life at home. (It would also mean less inflation and lower taxes, letting people keep more of their own money.)

Yes, there would still be bad guys doing bad things. But one country's military has no reason to be the world's police force. At any time, individuals who feel concerned about another nation's security are free to donate money to support those fighting for freedom in that country. They could even travel there themselves to enlist and fight. But abandoning the neoconservative foreign policy would mean that we would no longer compel taxpayers to fund these military interventions, nor would we send soldiers into foreign wars that have nothing to do with protecting their families at home.

Embracing a foreign policy of nonintervention—in other words, minding our own business and abandoning the role of the world's police force—is not without precedent. It was, for the most part, the express policy of the US government for a century and a half. That position was perhaps best stated by President John Quincy Adams (John Adams's son) in a Fourth of July speech in 1821:

> America, with the same voice which spoke herself into existence as a nation, proclaimed to mankind the inextinguishable rights of human nature, and the only lawful foundations of government. America, in the assembly of nations, since her admission among them, has invariably, though often fruitlessly, held forth to them the hand of honest friendship, of equal freedom, of generous reciprocity...

> She has abstained from interference in the concerns of others, even when conflict has been for principles to which she clings, as to the last vital drop that visits the heart...

> Wherever the standard of freedom and independence has been or shall be unfurled, there will her heart, her benedictions and her prayers be. But she goes not abroad, in search of monsters to destroy.

The tragic loss of life and the wasteful spending on the military-industrial complex have taken a toll on our hu-

manity, our freedom, and our wallets. It's high time we re-
nounce war and proclaim peace—and that means making
sure neocons never get their way again.

Tuttle Twins Takeaways

1. Neoconservatism has played a significant role in shap-
   ing US foreign policy, advocating for a strong military
   presence worldwide and meddling in the affairs of
   other nations.

2. Foreign military interventions, supported by neoconservative policies, lead to unintended consequences
   such as blowback, wasted resources, and the loss of
   lives.

3. Emergencies, whether real or contrived, often lead to
   increased government powers, which tend to remain
   even after the crisis has ended. This expansion erodes
   our freedoms and creates a chaotic political environment in which fear is used to further the agenda of
   those in power.

4. A noninterventionist foreign policy is not something
   new or unheard of; there is plenty of historical precedent for the government to remain neutral and not
   involve itself in other countries' affairs.

TAXES

History shows that letting the state coerceively take money from its citizens expands state power at the expense of individual liberty.

"Taxation is the price we pay for failing to build a civilized society. The higher the tax level, the greater the failure. A centrally planned totalitarian state represents a complete defeat for the civilized world, while a totally voluntary society represents its ultimate success."

~ Mark Skousen

In the early 1900s, local farmers attempted to divert water from the raging Colorado River and use it to help grow their crops. But when their canal plans flopped and accidentally created a giant lake called the Salton Sea, things got real messy, real fast. That's when the U.S. Bureau of Reclamation stepped in.

Arthur Powell Davis, the Bureau director, developed a plan in 1922 to build a mega-dam in Black Canyon, right on the border of Arizona and Nevada. They called it the Boulder Canyon project, and it wasn't just any dam—it was going to stop floods, help farms, and even make electricity to pay for itself. But, the price tag was a whopping $165 million, and that made a bunch of lawmakers and states nervous, especially since they thought California would take all the water.

Herbert Hoover was the Secretary of Commerce at the time, and he facilitated negotiations that got the different states on board by dividing the river water proportionately among the seven states involved. Finally, in late 1928, President Calvin Coolidge greenlit the plan and work began. A project of this scope was a godsend to unemployed workers in the area who flocked to Las Vegas, hoping to land a job. Workers had to blast through canyon walls to make tunnels in superhot conditions that were basically like working in an oven. At one point, they went on strike because it was so rough. Then, they had to clear huge walls to prepare for the dam, with guys called "high scalers" hanging from ropes, using heavy tools to break rocks—an extremely dangerous task.

The actual dam construction was like a massive assembly line. Workers mixed cement on site and swung it across the canyon with huge cable systems. They even had to cool the concrete with water pipes to stop it from cracking from all the heat. The dam slowly took shape according to its impressively engineered design, and by 1935 it was finished. Standing at 726 feet tall, a huge crowd celebrated alongside President Roosevelt. This monster of a dam used five million barrels of cement and a ridiculous amount of steel, and now it could water farms, power homes, and was even named one of America's greatest engineering feats.

That whopping $165 million bill? That was funded by taxpayers, without whom the dam wouldn't have happened. Or so the argument goes.

Next time you're in Washington, DC, head over to the Internal Revenue Service building. Facing Constitution Avenue, the building's main entrance has a decorative treatment including carved limestone eagles and an inscription that, in the minds of IRS agents, justifies their existence: "Taxes are what we pay for a civilized society." This quote, from a Supreme Court opinion written by Justice Oliver Wendell Holmes, conveys why most people think taxation exists: to fund the provision of services that allow society to function. Holmes was, obviously, a passionate proponent of this viewpoint. Once a secretary exclaimed, "Don't you hate to pay taxes!" He was quickly rebuked by Holmes: "No, young feller. I like to pay taxes. With them I buy civilization."

But is this true? Does civilization require the imposition of coercive taxes? Can no society be built without forcing its members to contribute?

The Context

Taxation is as old as civilization itself, which is perhaps why most assume the two are inherently intertwined. The historical record, such as we have it, suggests that early societies all had various systems of taxation to finance large-scale infrastructure projects, to stock the treasury of the rulers, and to provide the services demanded by the citizenry. The Egyptians, for example, taxed all kinds of things: sales, slaves, imports and exports, businesses, and foreign visitors. The tax levied on agriculture alone was a whopping 20 percent—and it applied to home gardens as well, no matter the size. They even had a tax on cooking oil!

To enforce these taxes and maintain compliance, the Egyptians employed an army of scribes who made regular inspections—going so far as to review people's kitchens to make sure the women were only using the taxed oil as opposed to any alternative. Surveillance was essential and everywhere; every taxable transaction was required to be recorded and was open to inspection by state officials. In this sense, the scribes were human equivalents of today's computer systems that provide similar surveillance of our financial accounts and transactions, allowing today's tax agents to monitor the movement of money and enforce tax laws. The Egyptians long ago, like us today, lost privacy and liberty to the snooping tax collectors tasked with keeping the money rolling in for the pharaoh.

All major civilizations have been managed by governments, and all governments rely on taxation. So taxes are not what we pay for civilized society—they're what we pay to the government that *claims* to create civilized society.

We are told that without the government, society will collapse; its proponents argue that anarchy and chaos will abound if the state were to dissipate. They further claim that without the ability to impose taxes, major projects—such as the Hoover Dam—are unattainable, and humanity will be left to languish without the benefit of transformational investments and improvements. This argument applies to all major projects, especially the most major of them all: war.

Think of the American colonists who revolted against the Stamp Act, among other taxes imposed by the British Crown. We recall their main mantra: "no taxation without representation!" But why was there a political battle over the tax to begin with? The Stamp Act was passed by Parliament on March 22, 1765, as part of an effort to generate funds with which to pay for military troops stationed in the colonies in the wake of the years-long French and Indian War. Charles Township, a member of Parliament, spoke in support of the tax to his colleagues: "And now will these Americans, children planted by our care, nourished up by our Indulgence until they are grown to a degree of strength and opulence, and protected by our arms, will they grudge to contribute their mite to relieve us from heavy weight of the burden which we lie under?" So went the debate, resting on the perception that the colonists were incapable incompetents, thriving only by the good grace of the Crown and its nourishing protection and provisions. Of course, the opposite is true: colonists weren't planted by the British but had rather escaped its religious and political tyranny; they weren't nourished by British indulgence but rather despite it, having to tame wild country on their own; and they weren't protected by British arms but rather took up arms in their own self-defense as needed.

Imagine Townshend standing behind the lectern, beating his chest: "This Stamp Act is the price the colonists must pay for a civilized society!" It's foolish, precisely because the colonists had been creating a wonderfully successful, civilized society on their own, without the burdensome weight of the British Crown resting upon them. In the Empire's neglect, the colonies thrived; but when Parliament wanted to fill its coffers, it utilized arguments such as these to justify them. These are the arguments that all tax-hungry politicians use. Why? Because they implicitly understand that taxation is theft, so it must therefore be enveloped in an alternative, emotional argument to justify its imposition and suppress any tendency among the taxed to revolt.

Why is it the Worst Idea?

Imagine it's late at night and you're watching a movie at home. As you lift a scoop of ice cream to your mouth, three intimidating individuals barge through your front door, wielding guns and shouting profanities. They hold you hostage as they go through your belongings and take what they demand. There's no room for negotiation, nor does it make much sense for you to point out that they're stealing and that that's wrong. (They're well aware.) How would you feel in this scenario? Violated? A victim of a crime? Vengeful? Consider an alternative question. What if, rather than invading your home, the criminals instead had access to your bank account and withdrew predictable, smaller amounts every couple of weeks? Would this be less objectionable than a one-time fleecing in your home? You might feel safer since you're not being threatened at gunpoint, but is there a substantive difference in the robbery you experience?

This is the conundrum faced by taxpayers. The state takes what it demands, and there's not much sense in pointing out that it's stealing. (The politicians are well aware.) And, like the frog in a pot of boiling water, the theft has been incrementally normalized—taken from paychecks and purchases in small increments—to spare most citizens the confrontation and conflict that comes from sending IRS tax agents to your door. But what gives the government the right to confiscate part of what you own? In a just and voluntary society, all property would be transferred through contractual agreement and mutual consent. By contrast, taxation involves the forcible transfer of property to the state with no consent given. It is theft under the threat of violence; those who protest the taking of their property will have their wages garnished, their bank accounts frozen, and armed agents of the IRS bang down their door in search of money they claim is theirs. "Taxation is theft, purely and simply," wrote the economist Murray Rothbard, "even though it is theft on a grand and colossal scale which no acknowledged criminals could hope to match. It is a compulsory seizure of the property of the state's inhabitants, or subjects." This is why it's the worst idea.

Many object to this characterization, of course. Beyond the traditional "taxation is the price we pay..." justifications, supporters of the status quo often query, "Who will build the roads?"—as if this is some "gotcha" that stumps those who believe that taxation is theft. To expand on the idea, some think that coercive taxation is required in order to fund so-called essential services provided by the state, such as roads—which facilitate commerce and enable society to thrive. Implicit in this argument is the idea that, without taxation, roads would not exist. This assumes, of course, that people would not voluntarily band together to fund mutually advantageous projects, whether a road through town or something bigger like a large dam.

Yet this assumption underestimates the capacity of voluntary cooperation and private enterprise. The historical record is replete with examples of private roads, bridges, railways, and canals that were funded and maintained without any government intervention. Even today, many homeowner associations manage their own roads, parks, and security services through voluntary fees paid by the residents who directly benefit from these amenities. This illustrates not only the possibility but also the effectiveness of funding public goods without compulsory taxation. Furthermore, the argument that roads and other infrastructure necessitate government intervention ignores the innovation and efficiencies driven by private sector competition. In a free market, where multiple private entities can compete to provide services, there is a natural incentive to improve efficiency and customer satisfaction, reduce costs, and innovate technologically—benefits often stifled under monopolistic, government-managed systems. And when the government controls the funding and execution of projects like roads or national defense, it predictably leads to inefficiencies and waste. The bureaucratic red tape, the lack of proper incentives for cost control, and the political maneuvering over project funds all contribute to substandard outcomes—and thus higher expenses for unwilling taxpayers. The competitive pressures of the market are much better at ensuring that only the most necessary and efficient projects get funded.

A World Without It

But what if some won't pay? Imagine a neighborhood of fifty people, and most want to build a park. Under the traditional taxation model, a majority of these residents can force the dissenting minority to pay for a park they don't want. In a world without taxation, how would this work? In economics, this is known as the "free rider problem," when someone receives a benefit for something they didn't pay for. Those paying for the park feel it's unfair for someone to use it if they didn't pay for it—hence the idea that everyone should be compelled to fund it, on the off chance that they in the future decide they also want to use it.

This nonsense is really just a lack of imagination about how to fund projects in ways that minimize the free rider problem but that don't require coercing everyone to chip in via taxes. People interested in jointly funding something like a park, or even a road, could by contract limit who can or cannot utilize it. Funds for major projects can be raised through crowdfunding and charitable donations, or by offering private sponsorships or naming rights to benefactors in town. Or, better yet, the project can be open to all, provided a user fee is paid. This is how general services are often funded, such as municipal garbage pickup or providing electricity to your home. People can pay for what they use, but this requires that they be able to opt out should they wish to not pay; no electricity payment, then you better have a solar hookup! This already happens on many roads around the country—toll roads, to be precise. Those who use the roads pay for their creation and upkeep by paying each time they drive across them. But even more broadly, roads are typically paid for via a gas tax, which is a clumsy way to approximate someone's burden on the road system, making them pay for their use. The benefit here is that if you don't drive much or at all—say, if you're a remote worker and stay at home nearly all the time—then you're not paying much. But someone who drives their kids around town all day every day is paying a lot more since they're using the roads more.

Want to get even more imaginative? We compared taxes earlier to legalized theft, and rightly so. A similar analogy is that the state itself is a legalized gang. It claims to control a certain territory, and if your home or business happens to be in that particular geographic boundary, then the gang requires you to pay them a fee to be left alone, or "protected" by their presence. This is called a protection racket, and it's nothing more than a shakedown by thugs. But this is what the state does. It claims to have exclusive jurisdiction over a particular geographic area; if your home falls within these boundaries, then it demands you pay up in order to be left alone—and that the money you provide funds their "protective" services. So if something like voluntary user fees is an antidote to coercive taxation, what would be the antidote to the state? Imagine a world where you weren't obligated to pay the tax collector who claimed authority over you. What if, rather than having a government claim control of an area of land, people who lived there could choose their own government? You can change your cell phone plan, your insurance provider, your preferred e-commerce service, your job, and more—all without having to uproot your family and relocate elsewhere. Why, then, shouldn't we be able to choose which garbage service we want, which security force, or which government we want to associate with?

Some government associations may offer education benefits, health care benefits, ample police and fire services, and so on. These would, of course, cost more, but people opting in to this association would truly be consenting, and thus their "taxes" wouldn't be taxes at all—they would simply be elective user fees they voluntarily pay. Other governments you could choose from may be more limited in scope, and thus cheaper to afford. You wouldn't get access to the network of local parks, or have child care benefits or elderly care perhaps, but that would be your choice, and you would pay accordingly. This concept is called polycentric law, the idea being that multiple governments could all compete to provide services to individuals, rather than each one marking its territory like a network of gangs. We all know that competition improves quality, lowers prices, and maintains a voluntary market of freely interacting individuals. Why wouldn't we want this same approach for how we govern ourselves?

Benjamin Franklin once wrote that "in this world nothing can be said to be certain, except death and taxes." Death is natural; you can't avoid this inherent part of life. But taxes are artificial and manmade—and though many have come to accept them as necessary to "pay for civilized society," it may be worth questioning if that's really the case.

Tuttle Twins Takeaways

1. Taxation has ancient roots. Major civilizations, like the Egyptians, utilized extensive tax systems to fund the ambitions of rulers, suggesting that heavy taxation had long been associated with the expansion of state power rather than the genuine welfare of the populace.

2. The narrative that taxes are essential for civilization overlooks the potential of voluntary participation and creative approaches to funding important projects that improve society.

3. Taxation is fundamentally coercive and is similar to being robbed by an organized group under the color of law. If someone takes 100 percent of your property, it's clearly theft. Isn't it still theft if only 50 percent of your property is taken?

4. We should envision a society where individuals choose their services and contribute to public goods out of consent rather than compulsion. This model promotes a shift from a society built on coercive taxation to one based on mutual agreements and personal choice.

GOVERNMENT SCHOOLS

Putting politicians and bureaucrats in charge of the rising generation's education has resulted in dumbed-down curriculum, mediocre results, politicized agendas, and a historically illiterate society.

" Schools teach exactly what they are intended to teach and they do it well: how to be a good Egyptian and remain in your place in the pyramid. The truth is that schools don't really teach anything except how to obey orders."

~ John Taylor Gatto

Born in Franklin, Massachusetts, in 1796, Horace Mann seemingly exited the womb with a desire to make an impact on society. This life mission led him to study law, but after opening his practice, he realized that the law was not nearly as impactful on society as was education. Why? Because the law dealt primarily with adults, and education was focused on the young. In Mann's words, "Men are cast-iron, but children are wax." He could enact social change best by focusing on the young. (This is an observation that all sorts of dictators and awful people have similarly recognized, from Mao Zedong and Adolf Hitler to Joseph Stalin and Kim Jong Un.)

After serving as an elected official for some time, Mann was selected in 1837 as the first secretary for the newly created State Department of Education in Massachusetts. In this capacity, Mann argued that all children should have access to a taxpayer-funded, tuition-free government school system. He wanted wealth to be distributed such that kids from poor and rich families alike all received the same education. And to ensure consistency in instruction and conformity to a centralized standard, Mann set up teacher training academies called *normal schools* to produce compliant teachers willing to go along with the new order of things. That order included observations Mann gleaned from his trip to Prussia in 1843, where he witnessed an education system focused on duty, discipline, and obedience. Prussia wanted a strong military and, for that, needed obedient soldiers, so they created a school system that would support it. Mann was enthralled with this fusion between the barracks and the schoolroom; he was particularly disgusted with the diversity of immigrants' cultures and languages and wanted to conform them to a single standard. "Those now pouring in upon us, in masses of thousands upon thousands, are wholly of another kind in morals and intellect," he wrote. And so Mann brought the Prussian model—obedience, conformity, collectivism—home to the US, where he quickly began popularizing its many benefits.

Like many social reformers before and after, Mann saw education as a vehicle to implement a uniform ideology and mold citizens into a cohesive, manageable group. For most of these reformers, it was a moral endeavor. "We who are engaged in the sacred cause of education are entitled," Mann once declared, "to look upon all parents as having given hostages to our cause." Families with their differing cultures, religions, languages, traditions, and practices stood at odds with the social reformers of the day. To homogenize the rising generation into a new order, those guarding the old would have to be set aside. And teachers would be the frontline ambassadors for this order, as envisioned by another architect of the modern school system, John Dewey:

> I believe that every teacher should realize the dignity of his calling; that he is a social servant set apart for the maintenance of proper social order and the securing of the right social growth. I believe that in this way the teacher always is the prophet of the true God and the usherer in of the true kingdom of God.

Oddly, Dewey was an atheist; his god was government, and the social utopia he envisioned schools helping create. Of course, not everybody involved in government schools since their inception has shared these activist perspectives. Most educators sign up for the profession because they love teaching and want to help kids. Yet, the system within which they operate was designed from its inception to prioritize uniformity and compliance. As the Illinois Superintendent of Public Instruction said in 1862, "The chief end [of government schools] is to make good citizens. Not to make precocious scholars… not to impart the secret of acquiring wealth… not to qualify directly for professional success… but simply to make good citizens." Thus government schools are, at their core, a Prussian-inspired system of producing compliance and conformity—a recruiting arm for the state to ensure its future by brainwashing the young. In this world, academics—though purportedly the reason the institution even exists—are secondary.

The Context

For Prussia, good soldiers were needed—and their school system produced them. For America, things turned out a little different. The model that worked well for the production of compliant soldiers, as it turns out, was also able to produce compliant workers. And this was a godsend for the business luminaries spearheading the Industrial Revolution since they struggled to develop a labor force of solid workers. For previous generations, artisans and farmers mostly worked out of their homes and set their own hours. Now, employers needed people who could follow orders, be punctual and sober, and do the same task for hours at a time in an assembly line alongside dozens of co-workers. Transitioning to this type of work was uncomfortable for many—the idea of showing up on time, taking orders from someone else, and often working in poor conditions. Workers' time was no longer their own. It was a new model that required a "new order"—one that the burgeoning government school system was able to easily facilitate. The same compliance required of soldiers was that required of employees. It was a match made in heaven.

Today, government schools are typically called "public schools"—a term that obfuscates what's really going on. These schools are not public in the true sense of the word. They aren't open to the public, nor accountable to the public. Instead, they are created, funded, and controlled by the government. Hence, calling them government schools is a far more accurate term. But they used to be called something else before the public relations ninjas started calling them "public" to increase public support for these institutions. For decades, these schools were called "factory model schools" since both the design of the school building and the processes used within it were modeled after an actual factory. It was a linear system, moving students through standardized information, regulated processes, and grade levels by age—akin to a conveyor-belt process in a factory. Edward Thorndike and other advocates of "scientific management" promoted the conveyor-belt methodology in schools. Their efforts were wildly successful.

But to be successful in producing good factory workers in factory schools, you need to treat humans like widgets floating across the conveyor belt—where children are "raw materials" out of which the factory managers create their "product," productive adults. At each step along the linear system, students are molded in a consistent manner from one to the next. Each station requires the product to be fitted with the same parts (standardized curriculum) as all the other products proceeding down the same conveyor belt. If a product gets ahead, the worker slows it down to keep pace and maintain conformity. If a product falls behind, a "special" worker is assigned to help the product catch up. And after each station performs its task, the product receives a stamp of approval and is sent off for sale to the market. This model of schooling—designed for an economy that is outdated by more than a century at this point—organizes knowledge into a linear arrangement where tidbits of information are transferred into the minds of students in standardized formats and amounts. The teachers, for their part, are like technicians on the assembly line, ensuring consistency in the products and performing the same rote task for each new batch. The student is seen as a "blank"—as in the case of metal, where pressure is applied with a mold to create a new shape, consistent with all the others going through the process. Thus, these extremely outdated government schools require all children to learn the same things at the same time in the same way at the same age as everyone else.

In this historical context, the birth and growth of government schools can be seen not merely as an educational evolution but as a strategic social engineering project aimed at molding a compliant labor force for an industrialized age. By adopting Prussian models of discipline and conformity, America's educational architects crafted an environment where young minds were not nurtured to explore and innovate but conditioned to conform and obey. As the gears of the Industrial Revolution turned, so, too, did the wheels of this educational factory, each churning out not just workers but also citizens primed for acquiescence. But what about the academic aspect? Despite the social manipulation and the scheming desires of the system's early architects, aren't these learning institutions still teaching kids who gain valuable knowledge that benefits their lives? Despite all their flaws, aren't schools still serving a valid and important educational purpose?

Why is it the Worst Idea?

These are important questions: is the juice from government schools worth the squeeze? Are they performing well enough to justify tolerating all the social agendas and cultural conformity? The short and clear answer is: no.

There are lots of ways to slice the data. For example, if K-12 schools were adequately educating kids, then they would be academically prepared for college, right? Yet one in three college students is required to take a remedial course—effectively a high school course you repeat in college. At community colleges, that number jumps to two-thirds of students. All of this remedial education costs taxpayers $7 billion a year—on top of the $750 billion spent on K-12 education each year. In hopes of attending college, many students take the ACT test, which has four sections for reading, math, English, and science. Points range from 1 to 36—with 36 being the highest score—and the final "composite score" is the average of those four numbers. For the past decade, the average ACT score has consistently hovered just above 21.5. In the past few years, that nationwide average dipped below 21 and continued declining. The average score in 2022 was 19.8—a failing grade at 55 percent of the total points possible.

These schools aren't educating kids well. Just consider Augusta Fells Savage Institute of Visual Arts, a government high school in Baltimore. Tiffany France was expecting her seventeen-year-old son to graduate in May 2021, only to learn his GPA was 0.13. You read that right—zero point one three. Even more jaw-dropping, he was ranked near the top half of his class. The school had 434 students enrolled, and only 2 of them tested proficient in math and English. As Tiffany said: "[The schools] need a whole lot of help. These kids aren't prepared for life, they're just not." And it's not because the school is starved for cash; at more than $17,000 per student per year, Baltimore's school funding is in the top ten nationally, yet 41 percent of the city's high schoolers have a GPA below 1.0. And it's not just Baltimore. According to the most recent Nation's Report Card, using data from schools across the country, only 31 percent of America's eighth graders are proficient in reading. Thirty percent are "below basic" readers—functionally illiterate. And only 27 percent of eighth graders are proficient in math—an abysmally failing grade.

There's another alarming statistic from the Nation's Report Card. They found that only 13 percent of eighth graders are proficient in American history. Ask yourself: what becomes of a nation when its citizens are ignorant about history? This is particularly important since history is full of examples of government corruption, abuse of power, authoritarian rule, etc. By learning about how despots rose to power in the past, we can prevent it from happening in the present. But that means we have to learn about it—and generations of kids are totally ignorant of it. Perhaps for this reason, the critic H.L. Mencken once wrote:

> The most erroneous assumption is to the effect that the aim of [government] education is to fill the young of the species with knowledge and awaken their intelligence, and so make them fit to discharge the duties of

citizenship in an enlightened and independent manner. Nothing could be further from the truth. The aim of [government] education is not to spread enlightenment at all; it is simply to reduce as many individuals as possible to the same safe level, to breed and train a standardized citizenry, to put down dissent and originality. That is its aim in the United States, whatever the pretensions of politicians, pedagogues and other such mountebanks, and that is its aim everywhere else.

He wasn't wrong. You can review curricula online that were used a century ago in high school, and it's material that most college graduates would struggle with. Government schools have dumbed down society, producing millions of ignorant voters who don't read much, let alone read history. These institutions are the worst because they have been so successful in transforming people into incompetent, apathetic robots, ready to follow the opinions and do the bidding of others. Of course, if you were part of the elite, this is precisely what you'd want. It's hard to rule over people who are historically literate, entrepreneurial, critical thinkers, and skeptical of authority. That's why the architects of government schools built an institution that produces the opposite—because the graduates of this system are, on the whole, far easier to govern.

A World Without It

As with many of the worst ideas, we don't need to theorize about what the world would be like without government schools. They are a modern invention, meaning that we can look to history for examples of how society can successfully educate its young.

Before the rise of government schools, education was a far more personalized, diverse, and community-oriented endeavor. Families, communities, and local institutions played primary roles in educating the youth, tailored to the needs and values of the individuals and their local environments. This decentralized approach allowed for a more natural, varied educational experience, where children could learn practical skills directly related to their community and cultural heritage, alongside formal academic learning. Education was largely a family responsibility, with parents teaching their children essential literacy and numeracy skills. For those who could afford it, private tutors were often employed, offering more specialized education tailored to the children's needs and parents' wishes.

In communities, churches often played a significant role, with Sunday schools providing both religious instruction and basic education. This system was not only highly flexible but also deeply integrated into the fabric of community life, ensuring that education was aligned with the values and needs of the community. And for those seeking advanced learning and experience beyond the basics, apprenticeships were a common feature of the economy, allowing youth to specialize in a career and pay their own way instead of racking up massive debt in hopes of paying it back in the future once gainfully employed. Hands-on apprenticeships provided practical and valuable experiences, creating pathways for young adults to achieve economic independence and contribute to a robust, skilled workforce.

Sure, in rural America and in developing nations, the educational attainment of young people was sometimes limited; kids were expected to help out on the farm at an early age, and families often couldn't spare the time or money to invest in their child's formal education. Today is a far different world. Poor people the world over have mobile phones, which open access not only to essentially all of the world's information for free but also economic opportunity as well. Information is abundant, not scarce; those who desire learning can easily find it, no matter their economic circumstances.

Imagine you snap your fingers, and government schools are suddenly gone. How would we provide education to millions of kids? Without taxpayers being compelled to pay for it, how would we fund it? While the past is instructive, so, too, is the present—and there is an explosion of innovation in education happening right now. From homeschool co-ops, uniting families together to share resources and knowledge, to microschools, empowering teachers to create their own educational institutions free from the bureaucracy and control of government schools—these and many more models present affordable, dynamic, and successful ways to help children learn and thrive.

Sometimes we can learn best by using an extreme example. In the case of education that might be the Sudbury model, started in 1968 by some libertarian-minded education reformers who believed that children educate themselves; we don't have to do it for them. At this school, the "students" are in charge; they hire and fire the staff. There is no curriculum of any kind, and students are free to spend their time however they wish. In essence, these kids enjoy maximum freedom. Some parents might freak out when thinking about allowing their children to do whatever they want, all day every day. Would they learn? Would they apply themselves and tackle challenges? Or would they be lazy and play video games all day? Well, we don't have to speculate. Having been in operation for more than half a century, the Sudbury Valley School has produced hundreds of graduates, many of whom were studied by Dr. Peter Gray, a psychologist and researcher. Eighty-five percent of the graduates surveyed for his research paper indicated that they were happy they had attended this school. "The biggest pros" to the Sudbury model, said one graduate, "are gaining independence and building a sense of self and knowing your interests." And these graduates have created successful professional lives as entrepreneurs, artists, musicians, scientists, social workers, nurses, doctors, and so on. Some pursued higher education and had no difficulty getting into college; many others launched careers without attending college. But over and over again, these graduates report high rates of self-confidence and gratitude for this freedom they had to learn in a way that was meaningful to them—honoring their individuality and protecting their freedom. (Government schools do not respect individuality and freedom. Quite the opposite, of course.)

A world without government schools is one where society can rethink what education is for—viewing it not as a rigid requirement managed by the state but as a lifelong, joyous pursuit of knowledge and skills that are directly relevant to individuals and their communities. This would not only cultivate a more educated populace but also foster a deeper sense of responsibility, community involvement, and personal investment in the educational process—qualities that are often diluted in the vast, impersonal structures of government schooling.

Tuttle Twins Takeaways

1. Government schools are a relatively modern invention, not an inherent part of human society. Before their establishment, education was a more personalized, community-oriented endeavor.

2. Government schools were heavily influenced by the Prussian model, designed to produce compliant individuals. Horace Mann and others brought these ideas from Europe, aiming to create a disciplined, uniform workforce, aligning education with the industrial needs of the time rather than the developmental needs of children.

3. Despite being termed "public," these schools are government-created, funded, and controlled, operating more like factories processing standardized "products" rather than institutions fostering individual growth and creativity.

4. Despite massive funding, government schools often fail to adequately prepare students for higher education or the workforce, as evidenced by high rates of remedial education in colleges and consistently poor performance on standardized tests like the ACT.

5. The focus on conformity and obedience in government schools comes at the expense of critical thinking and individuality, potentially stifling innovation and personal development in students.

AUTHORI-TARIANISM

Centralizing power becomes a magnet
that attracts the very people who
should least be entrusted with so much
authority to govern the lives of others.

" I'm not scared of the Maos
and the Stalins and the Hitlers.
I'm scared of the millions of
people that hallucinate them
to be 'authority,' and so do
their bidding, and pay for
their empires, and carry out
their orders."

~ Larken Rose

Widely regarded as the Great Emancipator, Abraham Lincoln is revered by most Americans and people across the world as a bold leader who was committed to the cause of liberating African slaves in the United States. Amazon sells over 10,000 books featuring Lincoln, and school textbooks teach generations of new learners how great a president he was for pursuing such a noble cause. One book calls him an "American hero," a common characterization from historians who often sing his praises. Here's one such description:

> Abraham Lincoln, the 16th President of the United States, holds a revered place in American history as a symbol of liberty, justice, and unity. Born into humble beginnings in a log cabin in Kentucky in 1809, Lincoln's journey to the presidency is a testament to his relentless perseverance, profound wisdom, and moral fortitude. His presidency, marred by the tumult and strife of the Civil War, showcased Lincoln's unparalleled leadership skills and his deep commitment to the principles of democracy and human equality... His eloquent oratory, including the Gettysburg Address, continues to resonate, encapsulating his vision for a nation founded on the principles of liberty and equality for all.

Those are certainly nice words to say about someone, and Lincoln is the recipient of mountainous accolades like these. Though praised as an emancipator, what few don't realize is that this wasn't his intent or focus. Sure, he denounced slavery as a "monstrous injustice" and felt it was immoral. But he didn't believe that the Constitution gave the federal government power to interfere with it. In a debate with his opponent in the Illinois race for U.S. Senate in 1858, Lincoln defend himself against a claim that he had supported "negro equality." Lincoln made his position clear:

> I will say then that I am not, nor ever have been, in favor of bringing about in any way the social and political equality of the white and black races, that I am not nor ever have been in favor of making voters or jurors of negroes, nor of qualifying them to hold office, nor to intermarry with white people; and I will say in addition to this that there is a physical difference between the white and black races which I believe will forever forbid the two races living together on terms of social and political equality...

Lincoln's goal was not to free the slaves or fight for black equality. His sole focus as President, as conflict escalated with the southern states, was to "preserve the Union." In a letter to a newspaper editor at the height of the so-called "Civil War," Lincoln explained:

> My paramount object in this struggle is to save the Union, and is not either to save or to destroy slavery. If I could save the Union without freeing any slave I would do it, and if I could save it by freeing all the slaves I would do it; and if I could save it by freeing some and leaving others alone I would also do that. What I do about slavery, and the colored race, I do because I believe it helps to save the Union; and what I forbear, I forbear because I do not believe it would help to save the Union.

The United States was founded as a confederated Republic—an association—of independent states. Thus, when the Treaty of Paris was signed in 1783 to end the Revolutionary War, the Crown acknowledged and recognized each specific state by name, noting them to be "sovereign and independent states." They were referenced in the plural, as in "these United States"—not a monolithic nation. And just as these later decided to join together via a new Constitution, it was clear that, as independent states, they retained the right to withdraw from that association. Lincoln, however, disagreed. In his first address as president, he argued that "the union of these states is perpetual." Secession was, in his mind, inherently invalid; "sovereign and independent states" that wanted to leave would not be allowed. They would be compelled to remain in the "union."

Of course, the southern states disagreed, which is why military conflict erupted. Lincoln's insistence on bringing these states to heel and compelling their ongoing association with the United States government led to the deadliest event in American history by several orders of magnitude. Over 750,000 people died out of a population of 30 million. To equate that with today's population size, that's like nearly eight million people dying over this question of secession—the combined populations of Wyoming, Vermont, Alaska, North and South Dakota, Delaware, Montana, Maine, and New Hampshire.

Mahatma Gandhi once wrote, "Strength does not come from physical capacity. It comes from an indomitable will." And Abraham Lincoln clearly had that. Using the authority of his office—and going beyond available authority when he felt so inclined—he pursued his course with conviction. Lincoln went so far as to suspend the Constitution and habeas corpus; launch a military invasion without the consent of Congress; imprison thousands of Northern citizens without trial; shut down hundreds of opposition newspapers and imprison dozens of their owners and publishers; censor all telegraph communication; nationalize the railroads; confiscate firearms; interfere with elections using federal troops; and deport his most outspoken critic, Democratic Ohio Congressman Clement Vallandigham. His goal was to preserve the union and to do so apparently at all costs. It was a moral end, in his mind, that justified whatever means were necessary to attain it.

In short, Lincoln was an authoritarian, and, as happens with most authoritarians, countless people who agree with the outcome have been willing to overlook and altogether ignore the means by which we arrived at it. In other words, people now revere Lincoln for freeing slaves (which wasn't his objective at all) and saving the Union while excusing his many unconstitutional actions along the way. As a member of Congress, he felt that the Constitution didn't give the federal government power to interfere with slavery, but once he assumed command of the executive branch—once tempted, like Gollum in *The Lord of the Rings*, with power—he didn't let textual provisions in an antiquated document get in his way.

Thus is the practice of authoritarians; dictators of all stripes often receive the praise of their heavily propagandized people. They, those in authority, get to write the narrative of what happens. They silence dissent, fund propaganda, teach their views to the young via the schools, and use the bully pulpit to broadcast their message to a wide and attentive audience. The question we must consider is: what attracts people to support and believe strong authority figures when so often these individuals are doing wrong in the name of doing right?

The Context

A recent poll asked voters, "Do you think it would be a good thing, a bad thing, or neither, for the next president to be able to take action on the country's important policy issues without having to worry about Congress or the courts?" How would you respond to the question? One in five individuals responding to the survey said that it would be a "good thing." Think of it—over 20 percent of voters considered it a positive thing to have the elected president do what Lincoln did, running roughshod over the Constitution's limitations of the executive branch's power.

The results were even more interesting when participants were asked the same question but with specific reference to the president being a member of their political party. If it was a Republican president in charge, a whopping 57 percent of Republicans said it would be a "good thing." Thirty-nine percent of Democrats answered this way. (One reason for Republicans being much higher may be that the question was asked while a Democrat was the president, perhaps leading more Republicans to want a strong leader to swing the country in the opposite direction.) Finally, the participants were asked how they would respond if the president were a member of a different political party. Seventy-six percent of Republicans said it would be a "bad thing" for a Democrat president to sidestep Congress and the courts, and 83 percent of Democrats said it would be a "bad thing" for a Republican president to do.

Clearly, people prefer authoritarians who agree with them and are appalled when the authoritarian is from another political tribe. People like it when their team is in power; they often see politics as a tribal competition, like a college football team, and want the other team to lose as much as they want their own team to win. The problem with this approach is that people become victims of the very power they support. For example, in 2013, the Senate Majority Leader, Harry Reid, a Democrat, invoked the "nuclear option" to change a long-standing rule in the Senate that required sixty votes—three-fifths, or 60 percent—for various votes such as judicial nominations. This required there to be more agreement than a simple majority, helping to ensure that decisions were reasonable and supported by more than just one party's members. Senator Reid was frustrated with this impediment and led the charge to eliminate it, enabling the Democrats—in the majority at the time—to get their preferred people appointed to various executive offices, with only the narrow majority of votes of the Democrats in the Senate. Fast forward several years, and the Democrats were in the minority. Now it was the Republicans in control, and they used the same power—a simple majority vote—to push through their Supreme Court nomination for Brett Kavanaugh. The change in the Supreme Court allowed conservatives to soon thereafter overturn *Roe v. Wade*, which proverbially set Democrats' hair on fire. But actions have consequences, and the flexing of authoritarian muscle by Harry Reid led to the same power being used against his political party soon after. The lesson? Never give your friends a tool you wouldn't want your enemy to use against you. It's one thing to love the authoritarian tendencies of like-minded politicians, but those same powers will be wielded in ways you don't like by others.

Authoritarian tendencies can be initially appealing. They often present strong, decisive solutions to complex problems—actions that cut through bureaucratic red tape and legislative gridlock. It's easy to see why, in times of crisis, or perceived crisis, the allure of a leader who promises to handle things quickly and effectively can be strong. But history teaches us that the power given to a leader to fix problems can just as easily be used to create new ones or to oppress. Seeking to address an "emergency" (whether real or manufactured), opportunistic politicians of all parties become eager to acquire and expand their authority to impose their will, like Lincoln did—and in the process, shape the narrative of how their actions are perceived far into the future. World history is one long record of the carnage and destruction wrought by authoritarians, from presidents like Bush and Wilson and FDR to people like Mao, Stalin, Hitler, and others. These authoritarians, combined, have caused the deaths of untold millions, with their destructive actions injuring and negatively impacting far more. Unfortunately, history also teaches us that, because of the way our brains work, we are susceptible to complying with authority figures as they pursue their agenda.

Why is it the Worst Idea?

Authoritarianism excuses evil in the name of some supposed "greater good." The person in charge commands something to be done, and those under him unquestioningly comply, whether out of love, rote obedience, or fear of being punished for noncompliance. When Nazi leaders were captured and put on trial for war crimes at Nuremberg, they cited in defense of their barbarous actions the fact that they were simply following orders. These participants in atrocities attempted to absolve themselves by blaming authority figures above them. To what extent were people willing to go to violate their own conscience in order to comply with an order from someone in authority?

That was the question posed by Stanley Milgram, a social psychologist at Yale, who designed an experiment in which participants were instructed to perform an act that violated their conscience: the administration of a series of electric shocks upon a person in another room whom they could hear but not see. Participants were told each shock would be more powerful and painful than the last, leading to a final, fatal voltage being delivered. Of course, no pain was actually inflicted upon the unseen person (an actor), but participants did not know this and could only hear the unseen person's increasingly intense screams of agony. As participants protested throughout the process, they were instructed by the authority figure to continue—that the experiment was important and required completion. Reluctantly, but compliantly, most participants subordinated their concerns and did as instructed, to the point of (in their minds) administering death to the other person. The Milgram experiment has been consistently replicated, with results showing that over 60 percent of participants will inflict the fatal voltage upon the other person when instructed to do so by the authority figure. Our brains make us susceptible to authority; we are conditioned by our nature to submit to the decrees of authoritarians, even when it clearly violates our own conscience. It happened for the subjects of Milgram's experiments, just as it happened for the Nazi officials going along with Hitler's commands. It can happen for you, too.

Authoritarianism is destructive; those who amass power don't relinquish it easily or reduce their status. They tax the people to finance their lavish lifestyle and send countless citizens to their deaths in far-flung territories in an attempt to expand the state's territory and thus power. They micromanage the affairs of a previously free people, imposing all kinds of regulations that require obtaining the government's permission. The world's worst atrocities happened because someone in charge ordered them to occur. Untold numbers of wars have been waged and people have been slaughtered—all at the behest of authoritarian thugs. Often these commands—stealing land, nationalizing industries, debasing the currency, executing dissenters, bombing other countries, and more—are explained to be in pursuit of some grand cause in order to placate the consciences of those involved. Entire nations and cultures have been transformed after an authoritarian's rise to power, leading a previously prosperous and free people to become a submissive, cowering citizenry going along with the authoritarian's agenda for fear of being caught as a dissenter. Authoritarians rule by coercion rather than consent. They impose their will on the people rather than abiding by the people's will. They undermine the rule of law, dispensing with any legal roadblocks that stand in their way. They violate individual rights, control the economy, co-opt the media, and crush dissent. Whether authoritarianism occurs in full, as in a totalitarian society, or partially, as in a constitutional Republic composed of elected officials, it is evil and leads to misery and death.

A World Without It

Authoritarianism occurs when power is centralized. Think of political power as a pyramid. At the apex of this structure, power is concentrated in the hands of a single leader or a small elite group, making it a singular point of control. This centralization is what fundamentally characterizes authoritarian regimes. In such systems, decision-making authority is top-down, with little to no input or dissent allowed from lower levels. This structure simplifies the process of asserting control for those at the top, as there are fewer checks to navigate and less opposition to quash.

In contrast, when power is distributed more broadly at lower levels of the pyramid—across various institutions, regions, or community groups—it becomes shared by many. This distribution creates a system of checks and balances, where power is not only dispersed but also counterbalanced by the presence and influence of multiple stakeholders. Each level or sector has a degree of autonomy and the authority to make decisions independently, which can lead to a more robust and resilient governance structure.

Decentralizing the distribution of power is critical because minimizing the concentration of authority is a safeguard against tyranny. In decentralized systems, it is significantly harder for any single entity or group to wrest complete control over the political system. The more distributed the power, the more points of resistance there are against potential abuse. Each level can act as a check on the others, and this interplay can prevent the rise of a single authoritarian figure or regime. Decentralized power also promotes a more participatory form of governance. It encourages political engagement at the grassroots level, fostering a political culture that values individual input and local autonomy. This kind of environment is conducive to liberty because it respects and upholds the rights of individuals and smaller groups, allowing them to have a say in their governance without being overshadowed by a central power.

What would this look like? How would it work? Again, history offers an example—most notably in the early American colonies where local citizens self-governed in town meetings to make collective decisions. They were able to manage their affairs relevant to their immediate needs without interference from distant authorities. Though subject to the King in faraway England, it was more theoretical than practical; the day-to-day lives of the colonists were hardly affected at all by the Crown. (Until Parliament and the King began flexing their authoritarian muscles, leading the colonists to revolt, of course.) Power here was decentralized, with independent and distinct colonies banding together as needed to share knowledge and resources. And even as these colonies became states and allied themselves first under the Articles of Confederation and later the Constitution, they were jealous guardians of their power and wanted to ensure that the newly created central government would not exceed its bounds and begin assuming authority it did not have. Unfortunately for us, as James Madison once wrote, the Constitution was but a "parchment barrier" that could not deter the ambitious politicians who progressively expanded government control over various areas of American life.

The Constitution's failure does not mean that authoritarianism is inevitable. It just means that human nature proves time and again how likely it is, especially when a citizenry is distracted, complacent, and ignorant. But this challenge presents an opportunity; a focused, active, and historically literate citizenry could reverse the course of today's governments, which have become increasingly authoritarian. It was because the colonists were so passionate and informed about their rights that they were able to withstand the consolidation of power and attempt to create a system that would protect their own. Their landmark experiment hasn't worked out the way most hoped for, but we can learn from past mistakes and build upon what they did. If we fail, then we can expect power to continue to concentrate at the apex of the pyramid, attracting the worst types of people who desire to use it. Like J.R.R. Tolkien once wrote, "the most improper job of any man… is bossing other men. Not one in a million is fit for it, and least of all those who seek the opportunity." The future of our world demands we try to decentralize power whenever and wherever possible.

Tuttle Twins Takeaways

1. Abraham Lincoln's willingness to suspend constitutional liberties highlights the danger of justifying authoritarian measures under noble pretexts.

2. The concentration of power at the apex of the political pyramid attracts those who seek to use it for their own ends. This centralization makes it easier for authoritarian tendencies to flourish.

3. Many people may endorse authoritarian actions if they believe these actions align with their political beliefs, but they oppose them when such powers are in the hands of rivals. This hypocrisy underscores the dan-

gers of partisanship in the evaluation of authoritarian governance.

4. Decentralized power, as demonstrated by early American governance and other historical examples, provides a more robust defense against the rise of authoritarian rule. It allows for greater participation and checks on power, fostering a more balanced and free society.

5. Constant vigilance and historical awareness by citizens are needed to prevent the rise and entrenchment of authoritarian leaders and policies, even if they are initially introduced for seemingly beneficial reasons.

NATIONALISM

Pride in one's country and shared culture can often devolve into a collectivist mindset that justifies hostility towards outsiders and suppresses individual freedoms.

"The higher a man stands on the intellectual and moral level, the less he is prone to nationalism, because he is guided by rational considerations and love for the whole of mankind."

~ Leo Tolstoy

We typically think of the European theater of war when discussing World War II—Hitler and his forces invading multiple countries and defending their conquered territories against the Allies' advances. And to the extent we think about the Pacific theater of war, it's usually only in the context of the Japanese attacking Pearl Harbor in Hawaii. But the Second World War involved conflicts large and small across the world. For example, in addition to Hawaii, the Japanese launched an attack on the Philippines, which was under US control at the time. They also aggressively invaded China.

Conflict between Japan and China had existed long prior to the outbreak of a world war, largely due to Japan's imperial ambitions. The small island country had transformed from a feudal society to a modern industrial power, leading to a desire by that nation to secure natural resources to fuel its growth. Japanese leaders wanted to establish the nation as a dominant force in Asia. And China, with its vast lands and resources, became a target for Japanese expansionist policies. This ambition set the stage for conflict, particularly as China was politically fragmented and weakened by internal strife.

On September 18, 1931, a Japanese military officer detonated some dynamite near a railway line. The Imperial Japanese Army promptly accused Chinese dissidents of being responsible for the attack and launched an invasion. This false flag event resulted in Japan occupying a northeastern part of China, a land rich in natural resources, which thrilled Japanese nationals who saw it as an economic stimulus to save their country from the ravages of the Great Depression. From 1931 to 1937, the two countries battled throughout mainland China; both Beijing and Shanghai were captured by Japan. And then, the Army marched 170 miles towards Nanjing. It was, in the words of one historian, "a nightmarish zone of death and destruction." Soldiers inflicted unspeakable violence and brutality on Chinese civilians who lived along the road, abusing, looting, and killing large numbers of people, including women and children.

The soldiers arrived in Nanjing and on December 31, 1937, began a widespread massacre of the population for several weeks. It was hell on earth—a reign of terror imposed by one nation's people on another's. Some 200,000 people were killed, with many more abused, tortured, and otherwise harmed. Nanjing was important for symbolic reasons, having been recently selected as the nation's capital. This horrific episode, now known as the Nanjing Massacre, is one of the most brutal moments in the history of modern warfare.

These atrocities were not random acts of violence but rather a systematic campaign intended to break the spirit of the Chinese resistance and demonstrate Japanese dominance in the region. It was the product of imperial forces and centralized governments dictating the actions of soldiers and citizens alike, using the crushing concentration of political power to steamroll over the rights of innocent individuals and local communities, all of them swept up in a tidal wave of destruction. And these actions were heavily influenced by the identity each side had developed, tied to their governments—the Chinese with theirs and the Japanese with theirs. This meant they didn't see people from the other country as humans; rather, they were dehumanized. They were cannon fodder and collateral damage; they were subhuman and deserving of their fate. This warped view of humanity—and the carnage it results in—is a direct consequence of nationalism.

The Context

Defined simply, nationalism is an irrationally strong devotion to the interests and culture of a particular nation-state, placing other allegiances as lesser priorities. It is the political equivalent of showing allegiance to one's alma mater—a passionate loyalty stemming only from where you happened to live and go to school. A nationalist also sees their own identity as intertwined with the government they live under.

Nationalism, as a distinct political ideology, began to take shape during the late 18th and early 19th centuries, spurred by significant cultural, economic, and political transformations. What before was a loose assemblage of local communities quickly consolidated into a variety of powerful empires and nations—centralizing control and perverting patriotism.

That's an especially important point to pause and understand. Nationalism is a distortion of true patriotism—the love of one's family, community, and way of life. These are natural and good; they are an expression of our humanity and our love for our kindred. When voluntarily expressed through persuasion and love, they are a positive contribution to society. But nationalism perverts patriotism, taking that natural affection and allegiance and tying it to a central authority—the national government itself.

Instead of a variety of voluntary communities with aligned cultural values, the nation consolidates authority, coercively forcing different people to pledge allegiance under the same banner, despite significant differences. The minority who dissents is forced to comply for "the greater good." The nationalist viewpoint was best expressed by the Italian totalitarian Benito Mussolini: "Everything within the state, nothing outside the state, nothing against the state." Individuals and communities are cogs in the machine of the nation-state; they can be disposed of as deemed necessary by those in power.

Prior to this centralization of control, countries were culturally based—a group of people who shared a common heritage, religion, and language. One's country, or nation, was a cooperative community of similarly situated individuals. And in that sense, patriotism is a positive—a group of aligned people working together for their common good. Consider the words at the end of the Declaration of Independence where the rebellious colonists, despite their various differences, "mutually pledge[d] to each other our lives, our fortunes and our sacred honor." There's nothing inherently wrong with cheering on the home team or wanting your community to thrive—or defending it from aggressors. Taken this way, patriotism is merely an extension of one's own desire to succeed and progress.

Consider the history of the British colonies in America in the 17th and 18th centuries. These were largely settled by small groups of adventurers seeking a better life, creating communities with people who shared their values. Many of them had been subjected to persecution by those in power and wanted to live amongst friends. Though under the King's rule generally, they enjoyed a long leash enabling them to self-govern outside of the heavy-handed control of the Crown. Separated by an ocean and after several generations passed, the colonists had grown to deeply love their communities and country; their patriotism was in allegiance to their people. This fierce independence and desire to self-govern had deepened its roots for decades. By the time King George realized the magnitude of the problem he faced, it was too late; a spirit of patriotism and loyalty to their own freedom had embedded itself into the hearts of so many colonists that they were willing to fight a war to protect it.

These colonial patriots rejected the long-held view that the government was sovereign and that its will should be imposed upon its subjects. They rightly saw themselves as sovereign and felt that they created their local governments to serve, not enslave, them. They experienced self-governance in their families, churches, and communities; they saw what power they wielded because they could exercise control instead of being controlled. They lived amongst peers voluntarily and ultimately decided not to be governed by those who were not part of that community. Thus, political independence was the only feasible option.

All of this is well and good; patriotism in a community-based context is fine. But in the modern era, that natural sentiment is twisted all too easily into nationalism. The rise of the nation-state has crushed the autonomy of individual sovereignty and self-governing communities. Where before people could move to another location and experience a vastly different order of things, now the entire nation has been heavily homogenized under centralized control. Community independence has degraded into community dependence. People's allegiance and attention and energy are tied to national politics and news instead of what's happening around them. Congress gets all the attention while City Hall remains outside our field of vision.

As the nation-state gains power, the individual is reduced to a mere statistic—an interchangeable unit whose value is measured only by their contribution to the national narrative. This dynamic fosters a dangerous shift in perspective. The heartfelt connection to one's family and neighbors is supplanted by a more abstract and distant allegiance to a sprawling bureaucratic apparatus. In this transformation, communal bonds weaken, and genuine cultural diversity is diluted into a sanitized "national culture" that often lacks any authentic local flavor. In an age where central governments regulate everything from education to commerce, "national values" replace the subtle mosaic of local traditions.

Why is it the Worst Idea?

Centralizing power—a basic prerequisite of nationalism—stokes arrogance and aggression. By its nature, nationalism evokes the spirit of the empires of old, hungering to consolidate more people and resources under their banner. Nationalism tends to lionize the idea of a collective mission—"national interests" that must be defended at all costs. That mission might be military conflict abroad, economic conquest, or the imposition of cultural norms on minority groups. Sometimes nationalism might result in all three, as in the case of Britain's and the United States' imperial treatment of Iran.

Mohammad Mossadegh became prime minister of Iran in 1951 just as his government was seizing control of the oil supply, which had previously been controlled by the British. Fearing a loss of control, the British reached out to their US counterparts to solicit help in stopping Mossadegh. The CIA hatched a plan to overthrow the prime minister and install the Shah, or king, as the absolute ruler of Iran. The project was named Operation Ajax and included activities such as bribing Iranian politicians, planting false stories in the media, and even orchestrating mob violence. (This is outlined in detail in our book *The Tuttle Twins Guide to True Conspiracies*.)

In early 1953, the CIA orchestrated a coup, partnering with supporters of the Shah to overthrow Mossadegh. The CIA saw Mossadegh as a threat to US interests in the Middle East, which included access to and control of the oil supply. Their plan to lead a coup was "conceived and approved at the highest levels of government." Mossadegh also opposed Western military presence in Iran and sought to limit their influence. He established closer ties with the Soviet Union, which the United States felt posed a threat to American interests in the region during the Cold War era. The Shah was seen as a more favorable leader who would be more receptive to American interests. Of course, it didn't matter to the US government that the Shah became a brutal dictator whose repressive regime attacked its own citizens. They got what they wanted: a compliant leader who would keep the oil pumping and embrace the US military's presence.

This is but one of countless examples of national politicians citing their "national interests" as a basis for deposing foreign leaders, stealing resources, occupying other countries, subsidizing friendly nation-states, and fighting wars. For example, President George W. Bush—someone whose administration repeatedly argued that meddling in Middle Eastern countries was imperative for US "interests"—used the same argument regarding Ukraine: "We should care about whether this young democracy survives because it is in our national interest... if Putin prevails, it affects us from a national security perspective and an economic perspective." That approach continued two decades later under succeeding presidents, whose continued involvement (and taxpayer investment) in Ukraine was justified on similar grounds. "We can't let Putin win," President Joe Biden argued. "It's in our overwhelming national interest and international interest of all our friends." And the Republican chairman of a congressional committee overseeing foreign affairs said that America's interests are supported by helping Ukraine fight its war "so that we don't end up in there."

Nationalists feel justified in getting involved in other countries because the decisions of those countries "affect us," as Bush said. This type of nationalism isn't just concerned with land claims or defending themselves against an attack; in this fuller expression of nationalism, proponents do whatever they feel is necessary or important in order to further the nation's "interests." In other words, if something can benefit the nation-state, then that thing should be done. The ends justify the means.

The core problem with this, as you might surmise, is that something like "national interests" is extremely subjective. Who decides what these interests are? What measurement do we use to determine whether they can justify getting involved in other countries' affairs? What are the limits placed around "national interests" and who enforces them? Of course, the answers are simple. Those in charge of the nation-state arbitrarily decide what their interests are—and these interests can change over time and for convenient reasons. They use no measurements other than their own mental calculations about what is politically feasible. Contrary to nationalist rhetoric, they don't represent the majority's interests—they instead try to influence through propaganda and impose their preferences on the masses. And there are no limits, because the state sees itself as sovereign and lets its leaders do whatever they want. Nationalists are therefore tyrants, using their political positions to impose their subjective will on others, all in an effort to advance the "interests" of the nation-state they control.

Rather than patriotic people seeking mutually beneficial relationships (like the early United States hoped to accomplish through a constitutional agreement), nationalist fervor prompts individuals to believe that their interests must be advanced—unquestioningly—through the apparatus of the supreme state. Such reasoning creates resentment and resistance, both domestically and internationally, as groups are swept under the mantle of a grand national project that rarely considers their unique perspectives—their dissenting voices either ignored or suppressed. Communities are crushed, figuratively or literally, under the coercive nationalist program.

This unchecked pursuit of subjective "national interests" inevitably leads to cycles of conflict and retaliation that not only destabilize regions but also cause immense human suffering. For instance, the intervention in Iran led to decades of animosity towards the United States, contributing to the 1979 Iranian Revolution, the taking of 66 American hostages, and the establishment of an even more anti-Western regime. Similarly, US involvement throughout the Middle East, South America, Polynesia, and Southeast Asia—and nearly every other region in the world—though justified as being in America's "national interests," resulted in a protracted conflict that destabilized these regions, led to the displacement and death of countless innocent people, and created fertile ground for savage groups to take root.

Nationalism concentrates power into the hands of the few on behalf of the many. Instead of individual families and small communities each working towards their own visions of success, millions are grouped together under one banner, with the state purporting to operate in the name of their "interests." Centralized power produces corruption and disempowers people who are unable to act on their own behalf; they are not truly represented by the government that claims to act in their name. This results in an identity crisis of sorts—though they share a cultural affinity with the nation and its people, many have diverging desires and thus do not feel aligned with or supported by those in power. One size doesn't fit all, yet political nationalism treats all of its citizens or subjects as a homogenous group. Patriotism permits a wide array of cultural and community-based organization; nationalism consolidates it all under a single standard. It's the equivalent of being forced to eat only one flavor of ice cream instead of selecting from among many different options.

Even worse, the nationalist mindset that prioritizes state interests above all else often leads to a dehumanization of those citizens who are seen as obstacles to these interests. This can justify a wide range of human rights abuses, from torture and extrajudicial killings to mass surveillance and the suppression of political dissent. The moral calculus of nationalism can thus easily accommodate atrocities, even against their own countrymen, if they are seen as necessary for the greater good of the nation, as defined by those in power.

Smart nationalists know that they have to be subtle about their aims; like a magician using sleight of hand, it's best to not reveal what you're up to lest you get caught. Thus nationalists typically call themselves patriots or other similar names to mask their true, opposite intentions. For example, after the Revolutionary War, nationalists deceptively called themselves "Federalists" and argued that a powerful, central government would better protect freedom. But *true* federalism required keeping government local in communities!

The true federalist patriots were slandered and intentionally called "Anti-Federalists" when they opposed this nationalist takeover. They expressed grave concerns about the proposed Constitution and cautiously agreed to it after amendments were added that would attempt to restrain the power of this new government, leading to the Bill of Rights. It wasn't long after the Constitution's ratification, though, that its limits were abused. From war and censorship to the creation of a central bank, patriots opposing the growth of this new government were steamrolled by the (false) Federalists and their ilk—the nationalists of their day. Wrapping themselves in a patriotic mantle, they justified their consolidation of authority in patriotic terms. And this tension between true federalism and nationalism existed until the poorly named "Civil" War, where nationalism became the victorious political doctrine in American politics, crushing the rights of states to self-govern and consolidating authority at the federal level via the 14th and 15th Amendments.

Since that time, Washington, D.C. has become overrun with bureaucracies, corrupt special interests, incomprehensible spending, and debt. Citizens living under this Leviathan are overwhelmingly helpless in confronting it as their wealth is squandered and their rights violated, just as the patriots warned. Nationalism fuels the growth of government, suppresses the voice of the individual citizen, and consolidates power at the apex of the political pyramid. Those in power can crush their opposition and advance their agenda, all in the name of the "national interest," whatever that means.

A World Without It

Obviously, a world full of billions of people will have developed different belief systems, cultural practices, religions, languages, and more—and society will be segmented along natural boundaries where people share common interests with others. In a world without nationalism, these natural groupings would not dissolve but rather function within a framework of cooperation and mutual respect, rather than competition and dominance. People would still cherish their local cultures, traditions, and identities, but these elements would no longer be tools for political manipulation or reasons for conflict. Instead, they would be celebrated as a central part of human diversity.

That doesn't mean there wouldn't be conflict, of course. But what adds fuel to the fire of inevitable conflicts and squabbling between different cultures and societies is the state—the institution that claims a monopoly of power and resources over a particular area. It holds itself legally immune from actions—even murder—and believes that the "national interest" justifies whatever it decides to do.

In a world without nationalism, the concept of "national interest" as a justification for overreaching or unethical actions would lose its potency. Without nationalism stirring the pot, governments would find it challenging to drum up mass support for wars or justify foreign interventions under the banner of patriotism. The reduction in state-driven conflicts could lead to a more peaceful international environment where disputes are more likely to be resolved through diplomacy.

Simply put, there are other ways of organizing society and other ways of thinking of ourselves and how we fit into the world. The idea of nations and nation-states as we now conceive of them is a relatively modern idea that would once have seemed bizarre and alien to most human beings 400 years ago. We can achieve our shared values and goals—peace and prosperity—without needing to wrap our identity in the state and become tribalistic creatures that believe our success requires others' defeat or subjugation.

Eradicating nationalism would require us to recognize that we have a great deal in common with people in other countries, despite differing languages and customs. We would see borders as simply lines on a map—helpful for jurisdiction and delineating different legal systems, but not a part of our identity. We would reject the idea that our nation's "interests" justify us meddling in others' affairs; we would be focused on ourselves, our own problems, and our own opportunities. We would be friendly and cooperative with others, recognizing that our shared humanity and desire for peaceful cooperation unite us on a level far deeper than any national identity.

And by eliminating the concentration of power under one nationalist banner, that power would be decentralized and localized—empowering families and communities to better act on their own accord and in their own true interests. Their civic and personal choices (wise or unwise) would yield direct and clear consequences, which would encourage greater personal responsibility. It would be a revolution akin to that of the Founding Fathers' effort, removing the shackles from an imperial monolith and instead creating independent, self-governing locales where people could easily move from one to the next to find the style and circumstances that best align with their actual interests.

By discarding nationalism, we could foster a society where cooperation and understanding prevail over conflict and division. Our actions would not be defined by the flags we wave but by the mutual respect and dignity we afford one another pursuant to the Golden Rule, regardless of what country we live in. A shift like this would mark a profound evolution in human society, away from the zero-sum games of political warfare towards a freer future where we elevate the importance of life, liberty, and the pursuit of happiness expressed by people associating with other patriots who share their values. This is not just a fanciful dream but a possible reality—if we choose to redefine our priorities and reshape our world beyond the narrow confines of nationalism. The future of our society is at stake. We've seen the carnage that nationalism can cause. The question we must face is: What will we do about it?

Tuttle Twins Takeaways

1. Nationalism has historically fueled conflicts by fostering an us-versus-them mentality, leading to devastating wars and acts of violence such as the Nanjing Massacre.

2. Nationalism is a perversion of patriotism, tying one's allegiance and attention to the state. It centralizes control, weakens communities, and robs individuals of their personal responsibilities.

3. Nationalism doesn't just involve pride in one's country; it often leads to aggressive foreign policies, as seen in the CIA's involvement in Iran during the 1950s to serve US national interests, which ultimately contributed to long-term conflict and resentment.

4. The concept of "national interest" is highly subjective and often used to justify unethical actions on the international stage, leading to interventions and conflicts that benefit a few at the expense of many.

5. Nationalism in a political context always involves

treating citizens as a homogenous group, which disempowers them and results in actions that are contrary to the interests of many of the people.

6. Eliminating nationalism could lead to a more cooperative and peaceful global environment where cultural diversity is celebrated and conflicts are resolved through diplomacy and trade rather than war.

CENTRAL BANKING

Giving a few bankers control over a nation's money supply inevitably leads toward inflation as they print fiat currency to fund the programs of the politicians they serve.

"History records that the money changers have used every form of abuse, intrigue, deceit, and violent means possible to maintain their control over governments by controlling money and its issuance."

~ James Madison

America's economy in the early 1900s was marked by rapid growth but also widespread instability, in part due to the government's manipulation of the money supply and the banking sector's overreach. From the mid-1890s to the end of 1906, the country's annual growth rate was over seven percent—doubling the size, in that time span, of US industrial production. Industrialization also led to consolidation; more than 1,800 companies were reduced to just 93, with large firms buying up their smaller competitors. Businesses were hungry for capital, and the gold-backed dollar was high in demand. This was especially true after an earthquake struck San Francisco in the spring of 1906, causing widespread damage totaling roughly 1.5 percent of the country's gross national product. As money flew westward to fund insurance claims and rebuild the city, credit was harder to obtain for others, such as farmers in the East who had a hard time securing loans to plant the new year's crops.

Part of the problem is what's called fractional reserve banking—when a bank issues far more credit than the amount of money they have on hand to satisfy their payment obligations. Imagine they have $1,000 in gold deposits. You might think that this would allow them to loan out $1,000 in credit to someone else since that's the amount of money they have that can be redeemed. But bankers conjured up a fraudulent system—fractional reserve banking—where they keep only a *fraction* of the amount of credit they issue. Using that same $1,000, they might issue over $10,000 in credit—under the idea that not everyone will try to redeem their credit at the same time. This effectively inflates the money supply and lets bankers be far more creative—and earn *far* more interest from more loans issued.

Let's continue with the story. In 1900, banks had cash on hand for only 14.8 percent of the loans they had issued. For years, banks had been providing credit beyond their means, and increasingly so—three decades prior, this number was at over 25 percent, indicating a healthier banking system. But by the turn of the twentieth century, the system was sick—poisoned by greedy bankers and a complicit Secretary of the Treasury whose actions supported the big banks at the time. And after Americans learned of some corruption in the banking community, word spread, and multiple institutions faced bank runs. On October 22, 1907, for example, the Knickerbocker Trust—previously one of the largest banks in the country—was overwhelmed with customers trying to pull their money out. As The New York Times reported, "As fast as a depositor went out of the place ten people and more came asking for their money [and the police] were asked to send some men to keep order." Two vans arrived stocked with bank notes, yet as this cargo was distributed to customers, it did not stop the panic. Bank officials worked their way through the crowd, hoping to calm their fears, to no avail. By noon, the bank closed operations. Days later, the bank's president, Charles Barney, age fifty-six, shot and killed himself. In the words of one journalist, Knickerbocker's failure created "a veritable panic on a continental scale."

That panic spread quickly. In the days following, numerous other banks failed as well. This became what is now known as the Panic of 1907; on top of banks going bust, there was an explosion of bankruptcies, industrial production declined, imports fell drastically, and unemployment skyrocketed. The largest financial publication at the time, *The Commercial and Financial Chronicle*, wrote that "The liquidation going on in Wall Street… is phenomenal. Stock sales… are among the high records in the Stock Exchange history." Shareholders were liquidating their holdings to grab what money they could amid the panic. The *Chronicle* continued:

> The market keeps unstable. No sooner does the optimist settle into a half belief that things have passed the dangers that threatened the industrial situation, and a few stocks, encouraged by that belief, have begun in a half-scared, timid way to creep up on a comparison with last year's smaller earnings and fresh promises of higher dividends—no sooner are these signs of new life in evidence than something like a suggestion of a new outflow of gold to Paris sends a tremble all through the list, and the gain in values and hope is gone.

Against this backdrop of economic uncertainty—and in the wake of similar panics in prior years—many in the banking community looked to Europe with jealousy and felt that what would solve the situation and create more stability would be a central bank.

The Context

A central bank is a government-sanctioned institution tasked with managing a nation's currency, money supply, and interest rates. In theory, they are designed to stabilize the economy by controlling inflation, managing employment levels, and smoothing out the peaks and valleys of economic cycles—precisely what the bankers in 1907 were hoping for. However, the reality of central banks is that this concentration of power over the financial system allows them to manipulate currency and influence the economy in ways that benefit politicians who want to create new money to fund their programs. Perhaps your parents have told you before that money doesn't grow on trees. This is true, of course, but central banks are the closest thing to it—they literally create money out of thin air to give to banks and the government to create "liquidity" and increase the money supply. This is the primary source of inflation.

But in 1907, the US didn't have a central bank. The country's history with banking was quite strained, to say the least—a contentious issue deeply entangled with the people's understanding of government power versus economic freedom. Alexander Hamilton, the first Secretary of the Treasury, championed the idea of a strong central bank. His vision was to establish a financial institution akin to those of Europe, one that would provide credit to the government and promote economic development. In 1791, Hamilton's push led to the creation of the First Bank of the United States, intended to stabilize the young nation's economy and establish credit, both domestically and internationally. But that word is important: *intended*. The *intent* of those who favor central banking is to create stability and support the economy, but the reality is often so different, and so much worse.

Hamilton's scheme in particular was not without its detractors, of course. Critics like Thomas Jefferson and James Madison argued that a central bank was unconstitutional and concentrated too much economic control in the hands of the government. They feared that such concentration would benefit a select few—particularly the wealthy elites of the urban northeast—while disregarding the agrarian and frontier populations. These critics rightly viewed Hamilton's plan as a manipulation of the economy that favored creditors, speculators, and industrialists over farmers, laborers, and the common man. The First Bank's charter was implemented but allowed to expire in 1811 amid ongoing political resistance. Its successor, the Second Bank of the United States, was established in 1816 but eventually met its demise under the presidency of Andrew Jackson, who vetoed its recharter in 1832. Jackson's famous battle against the bank was framed as a stand for ordinary citizens against a corrupt consortium of business and government elites, echoing the original Jeffersonian fears.

Suffice it to say, the banking elite were jealous of European central banks and frustrated with the rebellious resistance of the common American who was skeptical of such institutions. So after the Panic of 1907, the advocates of central banking decided on a new strategy—one that involved a high level of secrecy. That plan was spearheaded by Senator Nelson Aldrich, chairman of the Senate finance committee, who organized a trip disguised as a duck hunting expedition to Jekyll Island, an island off the coast of Georgia. This island had a fancy resort where J.P. Morgan, who was co-owner and a member, made sure no one else would be present. (Morgan was a key player in the Panic of 1907.) Aldrich—one of the most powerful men in Washington, DC, and an investment associate of J.P. Morgan's—invited a few New York bankers and the assistant secretary of the Treasury to this secret meeting and instructed them each to board a train, one by one, in New Jersey. Waiting for them there would be Aldrich's fancy private rail car, hitched to the end, ready to transport them on a thousand-mile journey to Georgia. Aldrich told each invitee to use only their first names and to dress up in hunting clothing to conceal their true identities and support the cover story pitched to the press—that Aldrich and some friends were simply going duck hunting. Some of the group chose new first names for their temporary identity instead of using their own.

This group of bankers, who together represented an estimated one-fourth of the world's wealth, spent the next week isolated in the Jekyll Island Club, working together to outline a central bank system that they could then get passed through Congress, using Aldrich's influence. Their efforts were secretive in part because Americans were deeply skeptical of both powerful banks and centralization of authority—so a "central bank" was hardly music to their ears. One of the attendees, Paul Warburg, wrote nearly two decades later that "The results of the conference were entirely confidential. Even the fact there had been a meeting was not permitted to become public." He added, "Though eighteen years have since gone by, I do not feel free to give a description of this most interesting conference concerning which Senator Aldrich pledged all participants to secrecy."

The plan they hatched succeeded; Congress passed, and the president signed, the Federal Reserve Act in 1913, creating a central bank for the United States. It was championed as a "lender of last resort" to provide liquidity to the banking system during times of financial distress. Proponents heralded it as a way to maintain public confidence in the financial system, ensuring the continuous flow of credit. And the bankers who took charge of it once created promised to "stabilize the dollar" and mitigate the economic booms and busts that had so severely affected Americans, both rich and poor. These are all wonderful claims and idealistic theories, but history shows it was a steaming pile of elite machinations that failed to accomplish the stated vision while enriching those closely connected to the central bank.

Why is it the Worst Idea?

Consider this stark reality: since the Federal Reserve was created, the dollar has been devalued by over 97 percent. Why is this? The answer is obvious. The central bank has only one tool available: the creation of new credit, or new money, thus expanding the amount in circulation, not only inflating its overall volume but also deflating the purchasing power of the existing dollars. As they create more money, that means all the existing money in circulation is worth less. The more you save, the less that savings can purchase over time.

Central banking represents one of the gravest manipulations of free markets and individual liberty conceivable, encapsulating the very antithesis of sound economic principles. Despite claiming to stabilize the economy and smooth out the fluctuations of economic cycles, the Federal Reserve's operations—like their counterparts in other countries—often exacerbate economic problems rather than mitigate them, leading to more severe and frequent financial crises.

These institutions are empowered to manipulate the money supply and control interest rates arbitrarily. These actions distort the natural mechanisms of the free market. Interest rates, in a free market economy, are determined through spontaneous order—the natural interplay of the supply of and demand for loanable funds. When a central bank like the Federal Reserve artificially sets these rates, it creates false signals in the market. Businesses and consumers make decisions based on distorted information; for instance, artificially low interest rates can lead to overinvestment in certain sectors (like housing before the 2008 financial crisis), creating economic bubbles that inevitably burst, leading to widespread financial disaster. And a central bank's ability to print money at will acts as a hidden tax on everyone. This inflation particularly harms the poor and those on fixed incomes, who find their dollars buying less and less as the price levels rise. This is not merely an economic inefficiency but a profound moral issue. It represents a stealthy erosion of wealth, disproportionately affecting those least able to afford it, without the explicit approval of the governed.

Central banks are a horrible idea for reasons that many never even contemplate. Consider their impact on the institution of the family. How, you might wonder, does economic policy set by the Federal Reserve affect families? Is this a stretch to tie the two together? Not at all. Let's first review, and then analyze, what economist Saifedean Ammous wrote about it:

> As the reduction in intergenerational inheritance has reduced the strength of the family as a unit, government's unlimited checkbook has increased its ability to direct and shape the lives of people, allowing it an

increasingly important role to play in more aspects of individuals' lives. The family's ability to finance the individual has been eclipsed by the state's largesse, resulting in declining incentives for maintaining a family.

Let's put this in layman's terms. When central banks and the government create new money and make yours worth less, it incentivizes you to spend your money *now*—as soon as possible—since it will be worth far less (or nothing at all) far into the future. To see how this plays out, consider a hyperinflationary situation, where the central bank is creating new money at such a rapid pace that inflation's effects are felt far more keenly than under "normal" inflationary circumstances. Under hyperinflation—in other words, when the central bank is really pouring gasoline on the fire—people become obsessed with the economic effects of everyday life, devoting their mental and physical energy simply trying to stay above water and spend whatever they can earn as quickly as possible before its value declines the following day. People search desperately for other ways to hold on to value, exchanging their money for something real. This surge in demand only makes it harder to find scarce, real resources; grocery shelves get wiped clean, and businesses collapse, unable to find the goods they need. Germany, China, the Soviet Union, Zimbabwe, Hungary, Yugoslavia, Venezuela, Bolivia, and countless other countries have seen a mass theft of the wealth of their citizens because of the manipulation of money, and the destruction of family life as intergenerational wealth is all but eliminated.

Think of it this way: in a system where you know your money will be worth very little decades from now, you are disincentivized to save. It's better for you to spend the money sooner while it has more value. To generate wealth over the long term, you're incentivized not to save but to invest—effectively to gamble, hoping that the stocks you bought will do well in the future and beat the rate of inflation. In this environment, it's unlikely that people will save money to leave an inheritance for their posterity. This creates financial instability within the family and deprives future generations of economic security. Quite the opposite happens: our posterity is left with massive debt, a devalued dollar, and an economic system so screwed up that they often feel hopeless and worthless. It's a recipe for disaster, and the central bank is the chief cook.

To summarize Ammous, devaluing money (by creating new money easily) makes people discount the future and focus on short-term opportunities since they need to use the value of the money before it declines. But what is money, anyway? It's merely a medium of exchange—a tool we use for collaborating with other humans. We buy and sell and make agreements with one another to enrich our lives and increase our prosperity. Money is really just a social lubricant designed to facilitate human interaction—a way to make our agreements operate more easily. But when that lubricant is contaminated, the system breaks down. Corrupt the money, corrupt the society. And that, in a nutshell, is why central banks are corrupting institutions that are harmful to our economic security and well-being.

A World Without It

In a world without a central bank, the economy would not be subject to the whims of a select few policymakers; instead, it would operate under a free market, responsive to the spontaneous order comprised of millions of decisions and actions. As with other horrible ideas, central banks are a modern one, and, therefore, we can look to history to see how societies can operate—and flourish—without them. When they prospered, these societies utilized hard money, like gold, to preserve their wealth. Government spending was thus limited to how much gold (a finite source) could be acquired. People were able to barter and buy and sell under these systems, and their earnings were not subject to a hidden tax by the inflationary actions of powerful bankers.

Without central banks, interest rates would be determined by the market. An interest rate is really just the price of borrowing money—and if the economy is doing well and many people want to lend out their capital, then interest rates decrease because there is so much capital in competition to be lent out to generate interest. By contrast, if the economy is doing poorly for whatever reason, then the risk of issuing loans increases, causing the interest rates to rise as well; if bankers are nervous that a borrower might default on their loan, then they are incentivized to raise rates to hedge against that outcome. With the market setting the interest rate based on real supply and demand, there would be no artificial booms and busts that plague our current financial system, which are often precipitated by artificially low rates that encourage excessive borrowing and risk-taking.

A world without central banking also means a world without skyrocketing inflation caused by creating new fiat currency that enriches bankers and funds the projects of politicians. Currency would need to be backed by physical assets, which would impose a natural limit on inflation; you can only dig up so much gold before it gets hard to find more. And because people's savings would retain more of their purchasing power, they would be more likely to invest in their future—saving for retirement and to support their children and grandchildren. Families would become stronger, and intergenerational investment would help ensure the financial stability of the rising generation.

Abolishing central banks would also drastically decrease the government's influence over the economy. Central banks create new money by purchasing government debt; in the case of the US, they offer Treasury bonds which the Federal Reserve purchases. The interest paid to the central bank is then returned to the Treasury. But the money that was newly created to buy the debt gets circulated throughout the economy, creating more dollars for the same amount of goods—causing price inflation and stealing people's purchasing power. With no central bank to purchase government debt, then, governments would be forced to be more fiscally responsible. They could no longer rely on monetary expansion to finance deficits without facing immediate repercussions like rising interest rates and taxpayer backlash. This constraint would likely lead to smaller government, lower taxes, and greater economic freedom.

As the "lender of last resort," central banks like the Federal Reserve are in the business of bailing out banks that engage in risky activity. A bank that is issuing loans to unqualified borrowers, for example, might risk collapse if those borrowers are unable to pay the capital back. If the bank's other customers try to withdraw their money, but the bank doesn't have it, then a bank run could ensue. The

Federal Reserve steps in to inject "liquidity" (newly created money) into that bank to ensure they have enough cash to operate. If central banks disappeared, then so would this moral hazard where risky behavior is subsidized and protected. Financial institutions would have to bear the full brunt of their poor decisions without expecting taxpayer-funded bailouts. This would foster a more cautious and prudent financial sector, where banks operate in a manner that truly reflects the risk they are taking on—like any company does and should in a free market.

Imagine a world where economic cycles are driven by genuine market forces rather than the arbitrary decisions of corrupt bankers. In this world, businesses succeed based on their ability to meet consumer needs—not their proximity to the Federal Reserve's money creation process. Individuals could save their hard-earned money securely, knowing that their savings won't be eroded by heavy inflation. Governments would operate within their means, and financial crises would be neither as severe nor as frequent as those we've endured in the past century. This is not merely a utopian dream but a practical blueprint for a system rooted in free market economic principles. The end of central banking would be the beginning of a far more prosperous economic era.

Tuttle Twins Takeaways

1. The economy in the early 1900s experienced rapid industrial growth but also faced significant financial instability due to government manipulation of the money supply and banks extending credit beyond their actual reserves.

2. Banks issued far more credit than the cash they had on hand, exacerbating financial crises when panics occurred, such as during the Panic of 1907, which saw massive bank runs and economic disruption.

3. In response to these recurring financial crises and influenced by European models, the US banking elite pushed for the creation of a central bank to stabilize the economy, culminating in the secretive Jekyll Island meeting, which laid the groundwork for the Federal Reserve System.

4. The Federal Reserve was established in 1913 as a response to financial panics, particularly the Panic of 1907, with the intent of providing liquidity during crises and stabilizing the dollar, though it has dramatically failed to prevent economic problems and instead contributed to them.

5. Central banking leads to manipulation of the economy that benefits political and banking elites at the expense of ordinary individuals, exacerbating income inequality and leading to inflation that erodes savings and purchasing power.

Hey, those substances will ruin your life. So I'm going to bring you to prison and ruin your life.

PROHIBITION

Banning something by law does not make it stop; prohibited activities shift to a black market where the costs and violence dramatically increase, making things much worse.

"Prohibition only drives drunkenness behind doors and into dark places, and does not cure it or even diminish it."

~ Mark Twain

On a warm June morning in 1900, Carry Nation, a six-foot-tall grandmother with a stern expression, marched into John Dobson's tavern in Kiowa, Kansas, determined to wreak havoc. Dressed in black and carrying a variety of household items, she began a violent onslaught against the tavern's glassware, liquor bottles, and windows, leaving a trail of destruction. Her mission didn't end there; she proceeded down the street, targeting other taverns with the same fervor, using billiard balls and cue sticks to amplify her assault. Nation claimed divine inspiration, asserting that a dream had commanded her to "smash" these dens of vice. Her unusual tactics caught the attention of the local sheriff, who, rather than jailing her, simply warned her against further disruptions.

This event marked the beginning of Carry Nation's fierce campaign against alcohol consumption in Kansas. Fueled by personal tragedy—her husband had died from alcoholism—and driven by a religious conviction to combat the social evils of alcohol, Nation took matters into her own hands. She became a notorious figure, storming into saloons with a hatchet, symbolically and literally attacking the root of what she saw as a moral decay undermining American families. Her actions resonated with many who suffered from the societal impacts of alcohol but sparked violent opposition as well, culminating in threats against her life. For her, it was worth it—a worthy crusade she had been commanded to launch. Beyond the active destruction of saloons, leading to over thirty arrests along with fines and jail time on multiple occasions, Nation published *The Smasher's Mail*, a biweekly newsletter, and *The Hatchet*, a newspaper, to further her cause and advocate against alcohol.

It was an uphill battle. From its earliest days of colonization, alcohol was a vital part of American life as both a beverage and a medicine. Drinking it was widely accepted and fully integrated into society. Decades before Nation's saloon smashing, a temperance movement had begun to flourish in the United States. It focused on abstaining from hard spirits instead of all alcohol, and on moral reform as opposed to legal measures to prohibit drinking. Advocates formed temperance societies to promote their ideas, emphasizing the moral, economical, and medical effects of overindulgence in alcohol. In 1826, the American Temperance Society was formed, and only a decade later claimed more than a million members.

By the 1860s, the temperance movement had grown substantially and also began encouraging a general abstinence from alcohol. The National Prohibition Party was formed to recruit and support candidates who favored legally abolishing the sale or consumption of alcohol. And in 1893, the Anti-Saloon League was formed to be the lobbying arm of the movement, focused on building political pressure in support of legislation prohibiting the drink.

Despite these efforts, the consumption of alcohol remained deeply embedded in American culture, presenting a formidable challenge to temperance advocates. The industrial revolution further complicated the scenario by accelerating urbanization and creating a social environment in which saloon culture flourished among the working class as both a communal gathering spot and an escape from the harsh realities of industrial labor. Saloons became not just places to drink but centers of social and political activity, often tied to immigrant communities and their identities. This association made the battle against alcohol deeply personal and culturally divisive.

As Nation continued hatcheting saloons, her tactics and the broader temperance movement's strategies began to diverge. While Nation favored direct action and confrontation, the larger movement—now with the formation and funding of groups like the National Prohibition Party and the Anti-Saloon League—increasingly shifted toward a strategy of political engagement and legal prohibition. Progress started in the states. Maine banned the manufacture and sale of liquor in 1851. It was repealed five short years later, but in that time, a dozen states followed Maine's lead. The Civil War in the early 1860s reversed progress and all but one of the state laws were repealed, but later in the century, the temperance movement regained steam. Kansas—Nation's home state—outlawed alcoholic beverages in its Constitution in 1881. In the years following, Iowa, North and South Dakota, Oklahoma, and Georgia also outlawed the production and sale of alcohol. By 1913, nine states had statewide prohibition and thirty-one others had laws allowing counties to prohibit alcohol, placing more than 50 percent of the country's population under some form of alcohol prohibition.

The Context

As events go, World War I was the impetus for pushing prohibition onto the national stage. To supply their soldiers with proper rations, Western nations established policies to manage food production; as the levels of food produced in Europe fell, people in the United States helped pick up the slack. The US National War Garden Commission, for example, was established in March 1917 to encourage Americans to create small "war gardens" to assist in boosting the output of the nation's food supply. One of the many propaganda posters said: "Food Will Win the War. You came here seeking Freedom. You must now help to preserve it. Wheat is needed for the allies—waste nothing!" And in August, Congress passed the Food and Fuel Control Act as an emergency wartime measure, which outlawed the production of "distilled spirits" from any produce, such as grain, that was used for food. Alcohol production was thus limited by decree in order to reserve resources for feeding the troops.

As the war concluded, prohibitionists used the prejudice against foreigners to further their cause. Members of the Anti-Saloon League, for example, popularized the idea that to drink alcohol was to be pro-German. At the time, many of the major breweries had German names, and by linking alcohol consumption to collusion with World War I's chief enemy, advocates were able to build support for their cause. One image created by the Woman's Christian Temperance Union to rally their supporters featured a voter stomping on an American flag while casting his ballot against prohibition. "The Saloon Backer is a Traitor to his Country," it read. Rhetoric like this helped use wartime patriotism to push for prohibitionist policies.

All of this culminated in a constitutional amendment to impose prohibition on the entire country. Passed by Congress on December 18, 1917, the proposed amendment aimed to prohibit the sale, manufacture, and distribution of alcohol in the United States—and being part of the Constitution, it would supersede and override the varying state laws that either banned or allowed it. By January of 1919, it was ratified by the required number of states to officially become a constitutional amendment. And one year later, on January 16, 1920, the law went into full effect, and the era known as Prohibition began.

Question: do you think that Americans stopped consuming alcohol? Obviously not. Many people stocked up before the law went into effect, hoarding supply to consume—since the law outlawed producing and selling alcohol but not consuming it. And distilleries and breweries throughout Canada and Mexico flourished, both from American visitors drinking on site and also smuggling their products back into the US. And because supply was (mostly) cut off, but demand for drinking remained high, a massive black market was created; bootlegging, or smuggling, was rampant as were illegal "speakeasy" clubs where alcohol was sold to those willing to risk it. Gangsters like Al Capone made huge profits from these illegal activities, satisfying the demand for alcohol consumption that didn't magically disappear once Prohibition was imposed on the citizenry. This lucrative black market enterprise led to warring gangs competing for customers, leading to events like the St. Valentine's Day Massacre in Chicago in 1929, where gangsters dressed as policemen shot and killed seven men from a competing gang. Prohibiting something popular has its very real consequences.

Enforcement was difficult for the 1,520 federal Prohibition agents tasked with ensuring compliance. But government agents got creative, especially in response to enterprising bootleggers who were stealing millions of gallons of industrial alcohol to convert it into a drinkable beverage. In response, the government secretly modified the composition of industrial alcohol to introduce poisonous chemicals like formaldehyde, sulfuric acid, or iodine. The president of the Anti-Saloon League was supportive of this scheme since, after the Prohibition law passed, drinking rates had not decreased. He argued that if people broke the law and drank poisoned alcohol, it was their fault. "The Government is under no obligation to furnish the people with alcohol that is drinkable when the Constitution prohibits it. The person who drinks this industrial alcohol is a deliberate suicide," he said.

Around 10,000 people died as a result of this intentional poisoning of industrial alcohol by government agents who knew that people would convert and drink it. This was one of many reasons why Prohibition was ultimately repealed just over a decade later, despite one of its proponents claiming that "there is as much chance of repealing the Eighteenth Amendment as there is for a humming-bird to fly to the planet Mars with the Washington Monument tied to its tail." President Herbert Hoover called Prohibition "a great social and economic experiment"—but ultimately the experiment failed, and tragically so. In early 1933, Congress adopted a resolution proposing a new 21st amendment to the Constitution that would fully repeal the 18th. This new amendment was ratified by the end of the same year—a clear indication that Americans were eager to reverse course.

Why is it the Worst Idea?

Prohibition died an early death in 1933, but prohibition lives on today. Numerous laws exist today that purport to ban behaviors that elected officials find problematic: gambling, prostitution, gun ownership, tobacco use, and the use of various drugs. Like with the legal prohibition of alcohol, none of these decrees actually reduce the perceived problem. Outlawing certain types of guns, for example, doesn't mean they disappear from the market—it just means they exist in the black market where, like with Al Capone and Prohibition, there is tremendous violence. Criminals become the primary users and distributors of the prohibited product.

Let's use the War on Drugs as an example through which to analyze why prohibition is such a flawed, horrible idea. Beginning over a century ago with the Harrison Narcotics Act of 1914, the war has expanded ever since through a series of additional laws that have prohibited more and more substances. The term "War on Drugs" was popularized after a press conference on June 17, 1971, where President Richard Nixon declared drug abuse "public enemy number one." He stated, "In order to fight and defeat this enemy, it is necessary to wage a new, all-out offensive." That took the form of more legal mandates.

None of it has worked. Despite spending over a trillion dollars on enforcement, these policies have not reduced access to illegal drugs, nor have they reduced the actual use of the substances. Addiction has not decreased. If anything, access, use, and addiction have all increased over the past one hundred years; drugs are freely available to those who desire them and are used by tens of millions of individuals. But the prohibitionist War on Drugs has indeed accomplished many things. To enforce the law, vast powers have been given to law enforcement officials across the country, whose ranks have swelled to fight the cartels and drug smugglers throughout the country. Police officers have been militarized to fight this war, producing tools and tactics—such as no-knock warrants—that have transitioned law enforcement from a peacekeeping operation to a wartime one. It has led to laws like civil asset forfeiture where, in the name of fighting drugs, police can seize your car, your money, or even your home if they believe that it was used to facilitate a drug crime—and they can do this without even charging you with a crime. And in addition to domestic law enforcement militarization and growth, the War on Drugs has also prompted political and military intervention in other countries, particularly in nations involved in supplying drugs, throughout Central and South America.

Just as Al Capone was created by Prohibition, today's cartels are the byproduct of the War on Drugs. Their violent tactics and amassed wealth would not exist were it not for the nationwide black market for certain drugs in the US. During Prohibition, bootleggers found that it was more economically viable to transport harder liquor as opposed to cheap beer; if they were risking their livelihoods and lives to smuggle a product, why not smuggle a product that would fetch a higher price? After all, it is easier to avoid detection by transporting less bulky but more potent items. Thus, Prohibition incentivized the production and distribution of harder liquor that people would not have otherwise purchased. Similarly, the War on Drugs creates incentives for suppliers to offer more potent drugs, such as cannabis with higher amounts of psychoactive THC or opiates like fentanyl, which are far more psychoactive. Suppliers are more likely to offer heroin compared to cannabis, for example, since heroin is over forty times more expensive per gram and thus a better sale in an illegal transaction. This incentive also exists for the drug users themselves; because prohibition raises the cost of the banned item, users seek more "bang for their buck." And since the overall cost is higher, they are more likely to seek out the more potent drug since they are already paying a premium fee. Both on the supply and demand sides, banning drugs creates an incentive to distribute more powerful—and more lethal—substances.

Both the heavy-handed law enforcement and the increased potency of distributed drugs have led to millions of unnecessary deaths, both from overdoses and in violent law enforcement encounters. In addition, prohibition causes harm by depriving people of the beneficial use of the banned item. Just as gun control can prevent a law-abiding person from having the means to defend themselves against an armed intruder, the War on Drugs has caused significant suffering by preventing law-abiding citizens from having access to these products for medicinal uses. For example, cannabis was prohibited as part of Nixon's war—a natural substance that has tremendous medicinal properties for people with epilepsy, cancer, pain, and more. Since that time, individuals desiring its medicinal benefits have had two choices: violate the law in order to use it, putting at legal risk their job, their gun rights, the custody of their children, and more; or suffer without it in order to remain in compliance with the law.

The Global Commission on Drug Policy issued a report in 2011 declaring that "The global war on drugs has failed, with devastating consequences for individuals and societies around the world." They were right. Prohibition in all its forms is an abject failure. These legal mandates do not stop the banned activity—they just push it into a violent black market and grow the government in order to attempt to enforce its ineffective laws. But prohibition is not just a logistical failure—it is a moral one. It is immoral for the government to dictate which substances a person is permitted to consume, whether it is alcohol, cannabis, raw milk, herbal remedies, saturated fats, etc. This kind of government overreach not only strips individuals of their personal liberty but also promotes a paternalistic state that believes it knows what's best for its citizens better than they do themselves. It ignores the fundamental principle of self-ownership: the idea that each person has the right to control their own body and make decisions about what to put into it.

A World Without It

A Louisiana judge authorized a no-knock warrant for police to forcibly enter a motel room, and within half an hour, officers stormed the room, fatally shooting an unarmed man and seizing a small amount of prohibited drugs. A St. Louis judge granted permission to police to break down the doors of three homes in a coordinated no-knock raid. Officers soon thereafter killed a sixty-three-year-old grandfather and seized a small amount of controlled substances. And in Houston, a judge approved dozens of requests for no-knock warrants made by police officers who relied on unnamed "informants" supplying them with information about the whereabouts of illegal drugs. One of the authorized raids led to a shootout in which two residents died and four officers were shot. The drugs that police were searching for did not exist, and the officer who requested the warrant later conceded that he had lied about there being an informant.

Despite a widespread recognition that Prohibition was a failure, many continue to support prohibitionist policies for nonalcoholic items, somehow thinking that alcohol was an exception to the rule. And what is that rule? Politicians cannot repeal the laws of supply and demand. Human nature is such that people who want to do something are likely going to find a way to do it. The government cannot completely stop people from behaving the way they want. All it can do is elevate the risks of engaging in the activity and thus produce a level of violence that previously did not exist.

Prohibition is a novel legal concept when contrasted against human history. People have always enjoyed various intoxicants and stimulants to dull their negative emotions and lubricate their social encounters. Societies of all stripes have to varying degrees embraced the use of psychoactive substances without the legal constraints seen today. You may have a moral position on whether it is right or wrong to ingest these substances or engage in certain behaviors, but that feeling does not entitle you to enforce your views on others.

Whether prohibition exists or not, these activities will still continue. But in a world without prohibition, they will be far more peaceful, less risky, and less costly. We will have a smaller government, lower taxes, fewer people in prison, and a shrunken black market. Those with drug addictions and behavioral problems will be more likely to seek help because admitting a problem will not carry with it a massive legal consequence. Addiction will be seen as a public health issue—not a criminal justice issue requiring police, prosecutors, and prisons. Gangs and cartels will be put out of business, just as Al Capone was over a century ago.

Yes, in a world without prohibition, intoxicating substances will still be available for those who desire them. But it is hard to imagine drugs being more available than they are today under the War on Drugs. A recent government-sponsored survey of high school seniors, for example, found that 55 percent said it would be easy for them to obtain cocaine; 85 percent said it would be easy for them to obtain cannabis. Those who want something can get it; eliminating prohibition won't change this. But it will drastically reduce the risks associated with the behavior.

While we can look to history for examples of how society got along fine without prohibitionist policies, we have at least one modern example to review. In the 1990s, Portugal was struggling under the burden of widespread heroin use; thousands of addicts roamed the streets as used needles piled up in the gutters. An estimated one percent of the population was hooked on the drug. "It was carnage," recalled one social worker helping addicts at the time. "People had sores filled with maggots. Some lost their arms or legs due to overusing." Portugal had been behaving like every other first-world nation, cracking down on drug use with increasingly harsh policies. But it wasn't working, and in 2001, the country embarked on an experiment by decriminalizing the consumption of all drugs. In the years since, drug use has declined; its prison population has shrunk; and taxpayer obligations have reduced. Those caught with drugs are provided with treatment options and support. Drug use hasn't stopped—it's just become far less dangerous.

Liberty demands that individuals should be free to make their own choices, even if those choices carry risks. The role of the government should be to protect the rights of individuals, not to infringe upon them through coercive measures like prohibition. We can privately encourage people to abstain from using dangerous substances without supporting policies that turn them into criminals for doing so. The world will be safer—and the government much smaller—as soon as we stop prohibition.

Tuttle Twins Takeaways

1. Prohibition does not eliminate the prohibited behavior; instead, it drives it underground, creating a black market that fosters crime and violence, as seen with alcohol during Prohibition and drugs in the War on Drugs.

2. Prohibition infringes on individual freedom and self-ownership, as it dictates what substances people can consume, violating the principle that individuals should control their own bodies and make their own choices.

3. Prohibition leads to an expansion of government power and a more intrusive state, exemplified by militarized law enforcement and policies like civil asset forfeiture, which undermine civil liberties.

4. Prohibition imposes significant social and economic costs, including overburdened legal and prison systems, wasted taxpayer money, and unnecessary deaths due to unsafe black market products.

5. It is morally wrong for the government to impose prohibition, as it promotes a paternalistic state that assumes it knows better than individuals themselves.

CENSORSHIP

Suppressing and manipulating information creates an environment where innovation and critical thinking are stifled, leaving society less capable of progress.

"Give me the liberty to know, to utter, and to argue freely according to conscience, above all liberties."

~ John Milton

In the spring of 1989, Chinese authorities were suddenly confronted by protesting university students and other residents who demanded economic and political reforms. For weeks, tens of thousands of students gathered in Tiananmen Square in Beijing to air their grievances and fight for reform. The government responded at first with warnings, taking no action against the growing crowds. In May, Soviet leader Mikhail Gorbachev visited the capital, and shortly after his arrival, around one million people flocked to Tiananmen Square for a demonstration against the government. By this time, officials had had enough, so the government declared martial law and stationed army troops around the city to restore order and quell dissent. But soldiers were unable to reach the square because rebellious citizens flooded the streets and inhibited their movement. Chinese officials ordered a heavy military force in response to take back the square. A report from the US Embassy in Beijing stated:

> At 0530 a column of about 50 APCs [armored personnel carriers], tanks and trucks entered Tiananmen from the East. Demonstrators shouted angrily at the convoy and PLA [People's Liberation Army, the Chinese military] troops in Tiananmen opened a barrage of rifle and machine gun fire. When this gunfire ended at 0545, a number of casualties remained lying on the ground. A second column of about 40 APCs, tanks and trucks entered Tiananmen by the same route and the students again moved into the road. PLA troops in Tiananmen opened fire with rifles and machine guns, once more causing a large number of casualties

Hundreds of civilians died and thousands more were injured. Thousands of suspected dissenters were arrested, many of whom received prison sentences for their rebelliousness. Some were even executed. After this overwhelming show of force, the protests finally ended—but then the problem began. Tiananmen Square soon became a rallying cry—a symbol of oppression by the Chinese government. This became a threat to the Chinese government far greater than a few disgruntled university students; the potential for this event to embolden others meant that it had to be contained. And so, naturally, the government responded by attacking the symbol. To this day, public commemoration of the protest is banned by law. The Chinese government censors any mention of the protests. Their massive surveillance apparatus and firewall controlling all access to the internet filter out any mention, and authorities swiftly punish anyone attempting to publish stories about it. On the thirtieth anniversary of the protests in 2019, media around the world published stories remembering the events; none were accessible to those living in China. *The Global Times*, a state-run newspaper in China, did publish its own story that day, saying that the massacre of hundreds of people thirty years earlier had been a "vaccination" against future "political turmoil," echoing the words of Defense Minister Wei Fenghe who said that the protests were "political turmoil that the central government needed to quell."

To restate the point, the *idea* of Tiananmen Square was far more of a threat to the communist country than were the actual *individuals* involved in that event. It is easy to put down a rebellion of unarmed youngsters; it is not nearly as easy to contain an idea. If Chinese citizens came to see the state as oppressive and themselves as deserving of freedom that was worth fighting for, then that idea—especially as it virally spreads to others—becomes an existential threat. Actions may speak louder than words, but ideas are far more contagious and compelling.

By controlling information, the Chinese communists aim to maintain their authority and suppress any movements that might challenge their rule. Censorship in China is pervasive, affecting every form of communication, including social media, journalism, literature, and even private conversations. These efforts are driven by the fear that exposure to alternative viewpoints and information about historical events like the Tiananmen Square protests could inspire dissent and demand for political reform. By erasing these events from public memory and suppressing discussions about them, China's government seeks to prevent the spread of ideas that could undermine its legitimacy.

The Context

Censorship is not something relegated to China or reserved for communists; oppressive governments of all flavors become tempted to control access to information in order to deter the ideas that can inspire change and resistance. In Germany, the Nazis produced their own propaganda to shape public opinion while also employing a variety of censorship measures—particularly in literature, art, and music—that party bosses felt were "degenerate." Joseph Goebbels and his Reich Ministry of Public Enlightenment and Propaganda helped facilitate the destruction of forbidden material; books that contradicted Nazi ideology, for example, were burned in massive bonfires. Besides the actual destruction of the specific books that had been confiscated, these events were a signal to those who possessed similar items—threatening them with substantial risk for owning, discussing, and sharing such material. They were as much an attempt to destroy the ideas in the banned books as they were to burn the specific books themselves. In addition, Goebbels's crew tightly controlled the news media to ensure that only state-approved messages were disseminated. And political pressure was used to intimidate those who might be tempted to disseminate information that Nazi officials disliked; a 1933 decree called the "Ordinance to Deter Insidious Discrediting of the National Government," for example, required Germans to report those who spoke against the party, its leaders, or the government. The Nazis understood that controlling information was essential to maintaining their grip on power and preventing resistance.

How about the Soviets? Lavrentiy Beria was one of the longest-serving and most influential of Joseph Stalin's secret police chiefs, serving as head of the People's Commissariat for Internal Affairs for nearly a decade. He coordinated the mass deportation of millions of ethnic minorities; oversaw the secret Gulag prisons for scientists and engineers; and managed the Soviet atomic bomb project, one of Stalin's top priorities. But after Stalin died and Nikita Khrushchev launched a *coup d'etat* to gain control of the government, Beria was arrested and executed by those who considered him a political threat. Beria, like other top officials, had been featured in the *Great Soviet Encyclopedia* for their loyal efforts to build the Soviet Union. After his arrest, customers were sent a new page to replace the one containing the Lavrentiy Beria article; he had been disappeared, and knowledge of his past role was to be dispensed with. Such censorship permeated the country; the government agency created to control information, Glavlit, not only eliminated undesirable printed materials but also made sure that what was published had the correct ideological spin. For example, the 1932 book *Russia Washed in Blood* shared a gripping account of Moscow's devastation during the revolution led by Vladimir Lenin to overthrow the existing government. In one passage, the author described "frozen rotten potatoes, dogs eaten by people, children dying out, hunger"—a passage that was deleted prior to publication. Anything unflattering to those in power had to be eliminated, for it might encourage dissent among those who desire a better life.

Communists in China; Nazis in Germany; Soviets in Russia. With examples like this, one might be tempted to think that censorship is a byproduct of totalitarian states and, therefore, not a concern for people in Western countries that champion free speech. This conclusion is understandable but very wrong. From its earliest days, the US has struggled to tolerate its own First Amendment, stipulating that Congress cannot enact a law restricting information. For example, as the French Revolution unfolded and Democratic-Republicans like Thomas Jefferson championed its cause—seeing it as an extension of the American Revolution—President John Adams and his Federalist allies were appalled and used their control of the federal government to limit French migration to the US as well as punish those who spoke out against their efforts. In 1798, Adams signed the Sedition Act, which made it a crime to publish "false, scandalous, or malicious writing" against the government. (Notably, the bill outlawed criticism of the US president and Congress but did not outlaw it against the vice president, Thomas Jefferson, the chief political adversary of the Federalists.) Numerous people were prosecuted for publishing ideas that were unflattering to those in power, such as James Thomson Callender, a British citizen who had already been expelled from Great Britain for his political writings. Now in Virginia, Callender wrote a book in which he called John Adams a "repulsive pedant, a gross hypocrite, and an unprincipled oppressor." For this crime, he was fined and sentenced to nine months in jail.

Since those early days, the government has, during flares of authoritarian exercise, been similarly tempted to censor contradictory concepts. During the Civil War, for example, newspaper reporters and editors in northern states were arrested if they wrote about opposing the draft or if they discouraged enlistment in the army; some were detained and others were exiled to the Confederacy. Telegraphs from battlefield reporters were also censored, and those appointed as censors had to screen messages to alter or omit those that could be "in any way injurious to the interest of the government"—a ridiculously broad mandate. A decade later, Congress passed the Comstock Act, which permitted the United States Postal Service to search people's mail, without a warrant, for anything "obscene, lewd, lascivious, indecent, or immoral"—but the law contained no definitions for these terms, leaving its interpretation up to those empowered to censor people's private letters, books, and other mailed material. During World War I, President Woodrow Wilson signed a new Sedition Act, making it a crime to "willfully utter, print, write, or publish any disloyal, profane, scurrilous, or abusive language about the form of the Government of the United States." The law was used to punish those who opposed US involvement in the war, with more than a thousand people being prosecuted. And in 1971, when *The New York Times* published the Pentagon Papers—a series of documents that revealed the government's lies about its involvement in the Vietnam War—President Nixon and his attorney general obtained a federal court injunction, forcing the paper to stop publishing additional information using the confidential documents.

More recently, the government has engaged in censorship to: suppress unflattering narratives about its response to COVID-19; suppress a true story about Hunter Biden's laptop in order to boost Joe Biden's electoral chances; attack so-called "misinformation" and "disinformation"—ideas that challenge the ruling elite's narratives; punish truth-tellers like Julian Assange and Edward Snowden who, at great personal risk, shared state secrets that reveal corruption; and pressure social media companies to manipulate their users' experiences in order to limit access to information the government considers problematic. Whether in totalitarian states or democratic nations, the impulse to control information arises from the fear that free thought and open discourse could inspire resistance to the status quo. And while physical force can suppress individuals, controlling the spread of ideas requires constant vigilance and extensive resources—a massive government with oppressive laws and a vast network of enforcement officers to see it through. This battle between those in power and the free flow of information is fought here at home as much as it is abroad and demonstrates that the fight for truth is far from over.

Why is it the Worst Idea?

In April 2022, the Under-Secretary-General for Global Communications at the United Nations, Melissa Fleming, proudly announced a partnership with Google to manipulate what people see when using the popular search engine to research climate change. Fleming boasted that, as a result of this initiative, users "will find authoritative information from the United Nations" in order "to ensure that factual, trustworthy content about climate is available to as wide a global audience as possible." Of course, what politicians and bureaucrats call "factual, trustworthy content" is often false information—and what they call "misinformation" is often true but in conflict with their plans and desires.

Censorship is effective whether it's done by the state's agents directly or in "partnership" between the state and the private sector—such as social media companies colluding with the federal government to suppress true-but-unpopular information about COVID-19. Our tech-enabled world presents both a challenge and an opportunity with censorship. The opportunity is that each of us can be a citizen journalist, seeking out and sharing truthful information with others using a variety of online platforms that make it easy to publish ideas. The challenge is that the more popular publishing sites are centralized under the control of a few corporations, the owners and employees of which are heavily supportive of leftist Democrats. And this is why they are so open to using their platforms to censor on behalf of the state; a recent poll by Pew Research Center found that 65 percent of Democrats agreed that "The US government should take steps to restrict false information online, even if it limits freedom of information."

It is difficult to understate how awful censorship is and the breadth of negative effects it necessarily causes. At its core, censorship violates free speech, which is a foundational prerequisite of a free society; as famed author George Orwell said, "If liberty means anything at all, it means the right to tell people what they do not want to hear." Suppressing ideas that challenge those in power leads to a tyrannical state and empowers the elite to impose their evil designs on the masses. Another reason why censorship is a horrible idea is that it suppresses truth, preventing factual information from competing in a marketplace of ideas. When the government puts its finger on the scale, it leads people to believe certain things are correct simply because officials said so—not because they critically evaluated the idea in contrast to competing ideas. History is full of examples of government officials lying or simply being wrong; when they impose these bad ideas on others and give them an official stamp of approval, they are preventing the free flow of ideas that will allow the truth to be identified and embraced by the majority of people.

There are many more reasons why censorship is evil. Let's briefly review a few of them.

- Censorship inhibits knowledge. Restricting access to information impedes intellectual growth by denying people the ability to understand truth. This imposes a ceiling or limit on the amount of knowledge a person can gain, arbitrarily put in place by government officials who want to hide certain information from the public.

- Censorship stifles innovation. When information is restricted, individuals are denied access to diverging perspectives and critical feedback, which is essential for creative and scientific breakthroughs. If those in power punish people who challenge approved ideas, then they will be unlikely to challenge those ideas in pursuit of discovering new truths. Censorship effectively puts a brake on the creative processes that drive technological advancements and societal improvements.

- Censorship grows the government. When those in power try to control and manipulate information, they enlist in their cause vast numbers of enforcement agents to carry out their censorious designs. This expansion of government power often extends beyond just suppressing dissenting voices to intruding into other aspects of our lives—leading to surveillance, mass data collection, propaganda, police militarization, and more. When governments censor, they set a precedent for further encroachments on individual rights, leading to an increasingly authoritarian state.

- Censorship erodes individual autonomy. Suppressing certain ideas strips people of their ability to think independently and make informed decisions. It imposes a one-sided narrative that people accept without question since they have no contradictory information that would lead them to believe differently. By controlling what information is accessible, governments that engage in censorship dictate what is considered true or acceptable, effectively turning citizens into passive recipients of information rather than active, critical thinkers.

As the Cold War heated up, President Harry Truman delivered a message to Congress on August 8, 1950, where he rightly warned that "Once a government is committed to the principle of silencing the voice of opposition, it has only one way to go, and that is down the path of increasingly repressive measures, until it becomes a source of terror to all its citizens and creates a country where everyone lives in fear." This aptly summarizes totalitarian regimes throughout history that have engaged in heavy censorship; whenever the government attempts to stifle dissent and shape a particular narrative by restricting the flow of information, tyranny always follows.

A World Without It

The French Revolution was a movement against the established ruling class in France, but the ideas that fueled it radiated across Europe. In Britain, a number of English political thinkers developed a reform movement of their own; at the time, the nobility dominated both houses of Parliament, and very few people had the right to vote. The famous pamphleteer Thomas Paine was part of the effort and, in 1791, published *The Rights of Man*, which criticized the British government and monarchy, arguing for a more just and equal society. Paine condemned monarchy and argued that revolution is permissible when a government does not safeguard the natural rights of its people. Naturally, the ruling political class disfavors those who rile up the citizenry to revolt against them, and such was the case in Britain. Paine's publication made him a target of the authorities; George III issued a Royal Proclamation Against Seditious Writings and Publications just a few months after it was published. Writers, printers, and publishers were arrested and prosecuted for treason. Paine, for his part, had fled to France and, therefore, was tried *in absentia* and convicted of seditious libel against the Crown. Had he been in England still, he would have been hanged.

The Crown's censorship of controversial ideas stands in contrast to Paine's previous writings and their impact on the King's former colonies. In 1776, Paine anonymously published *Common Sense*, a powerful pamphlet advocating for American independence from Britain. Its straightforward arguments and passionate rhetoric resonated deeply with most colonists, fueling the revolutionary spirit that later spilled over into revolution. These ideas—these *uncensored* ideas—spread virally throughout the colonies, emboldening many who soon became the country's greatest patriots and political architects. *Common Sense* demonstrates the profound impact that free-flowing ideas can have on society. By challenging the legitimacy of British rule and advocating for self-governance, Paine inspired colonists to envision a future free from tyranny— to envision a different world that would require a radical departure from the status quo and those who enforced it. The pamphlet's widespread dissemination shows the power of unfiltered ideas to mobilize people and bring about significant change.

A world without government censorship would be a world where our rights were protected and political power was decentralized. Any concentration of authority into a centralized government empowers those in charge to use censorship as a tool to quell dissent and maintain their power. Eliminating censorship therefore requires dismantling the state and returning power to the people. In that utopia, open discourse would flourish, allowing individuals to freely debate and discuss ideas without fear of reprisal. And because power would be more localized, any one person would not have a significant influence when attempting to censor, as they would not be able to affect the operations of publishers, editors, or entire media outlets. Thus, a world without censorship would be a broader signal that the world has a greater degree of freedom than in times past, living under large dictatorships and democracies.

The philosopher and acclaimed author Ayn Rand once wrote that the lust for power "is a weed that grows only in the vacant lots of an abandoned mind." This is an accurate indictment of those who seek power over others, but it also hints at the fact that those who seek power to rule over others want an uninformed populace, their minds filled with superstitions and frivolities to distract them from understanding the truth. It's easier to govern stupid people than smart ones. Here we see why censorship is so tempting: by suppressing ideas that are hostile to your carefully managed status quo, you can better ensure that it continues as you desire. You're effectively removing intellectual obstacles that impede your path to success. Put simply, censors are tyrants whose primary goal is preserving and increasing their own power.

So who wouldn't want a world without tyrants? (Other than the tyrants.) To continue with Rand's theme, imagine a home with a beautiful front yard that includes a lush, green lawn. That lawn's strength comes from hundreds of thousands of tiny grass blades, each occupying its own space and strengthening the blades around it in a vast network of roots. In this situation, it is very difficult for a weed to enter and take root; only when the grass becomes thinned from poor management—such as failing to provide enough water—can a weed seed find a dry, sparse spot where it will thrive. Similarly, a free and open marketplace of ideas creates a strong social fabric where concepts can be evaluated, debated, implemented, and discarded as needed. Truth is like the network of grass roots, but if open spots are created through neglect or brute force (*i.e.*, ripping out a section of lawn or forcibly censoring certain ideas), then intellectual weeds and power lust can enter.

It's not hard to imagine the virtuous cycle that would be created in the absence of government censorship. The freedom to access and share ideas—including controversial ones—would lead to a more enlightened and informed populace. We could engage in open and honest discourse with all the facts rather than having some information suppressed or eliminated; journalists could openly report the information they come across without the fear of reprisal. An unrestricted exchange of ideas would drive innovation and creativity. And perhaps most importantly, people would have the tools necessary to hold their leaders accountable to reduce corruption and decentralize power to smaller levels of governance. We would have a more honest education system that can share all the facts, producing critical thinkers who are difficult for despots to rule over. In short, a world without censorship would be a world of freedom.

Tuttle Twins Takeaways

1. Ideas that challenge the status quo are more threatening to oppressive regimes than even physical protests. Controlling information helps maintain power.

2. Censorship by governments, whether totalitarian or democratic, suppresses dissent, protects authority, and impedes societal progress.

3. All types of government engage in censorship whether they are dictatorships or democracies. The concentration of power, in any form of government, creates a temptation to suppress ideas that threaten that power.

4. Modern technology enables both the spread of information and its censorship, with centralized platforms often collaborating with governments.

5. Censorship stifles innovation, creativity, and critical thinking by limiting access to diverse ideas that challenge the status quo.

6. Free access to information is essential for holding people in power accountable and reducing corruption.

CONSCRIPTION

Forcing individuals into military service against their will is a violation of personal freedom, akin to state-sanctioned slavery.

"Where is it written in the Constitution, in what article or section is it contained, that you may take children from their parents, and parents from their children, and compel them to fight the battles of any war in which the folly or the wickedness of government may engage it?"

~ Daniel Webster

You know about the Civil War—the fight between the states, instigated by Abraham Lincoln in order to quash the southern states' secession and keep the Union intact. But did you know that there was a civil war within the Civil War? It happened in Lower Manhattan, New York, in July 1863. For years, the city had become a magnet for immigrants, particularly from Ireland and Germany. And the political machine in New York worked hard to help these immigrants become citizens in order to bolster their electoral chances. But these new citizens quickly discovered that they were being sought after as cannon fodder, subject to a newly enacted conscription law passed by Congress just a few weeks prior. The Civil War Military Draft Act became the first national conscription law in the United States, requiring every male citizen—and all immigrants who simply had *filed* for citizenship—between the ages of twenty and forty-five to enroll themselves for a military assignment.

On July 13, 1863, just ten days after the Union victory at Gettysburg, 500 angry immigrants stormed the provost marshal's office where the draft was taking place. The crowd threw large stones through windows and lit the building on fire. The destruction spread from there, with the mob smashing cars, killing horses, and assaulting people. When the police superintendent showed up, he was attacked and left nearly unconscious. Physicians later counted over seventy knife wounds in his body. The police force that responded was overwhelmed and unable to stop the riots, which spread to other buildings such as the nearby hotel and two police stations. Rioters targeted the office of *The New York Times* but were repelled by newspaper staff manning large machine guns; *Times* founder Henry

Raymond was among the group defending their property.

The federal government sent troops in to suppress the riots; some 4,000 soldiers were pulled out of the Gettysburg campaign to assist. By the time they succeeded, days after the riots first began, more than fifty buildings had been burned to the ground. Over 2,000 people had been injured, and hundreds had died. The Draft Riot of 1863, as it's now known, remains one of the deadliest episodes of civil unrest in American history. While the civil war within the Civil War had ended, conscription continued both in the North and the South. The Union compelled 168,649 men to join the Army as part of their draft, while the Confederacy is estimated to have drafted somewhere over 100,000. Conscription was understandably unpopular; in the North, over 120,000 men evaded it, and at least 100,000 men in the South. Hundreds of thousands of conscripted soldiers deserted during the war.

The impact of conscription extended beyond the battlefield. It disrupted families, pulling men from their homes and leaving many women to manage farms and businesses alone. The absence of so many men led to labor shortages and economic difficulties, compounding the hardships of a region already strained by war. This disruption was felt acutely in small, close-knit communities where every able-bodied man was crucial to the local economy and way of life. The Civil War was the first time the United States had implemented a draft on a national scale, but it wouldn't be the last time. Around the world and throughout history, governments have found it necessary or simply politically expedient to implement coercive military enlistment in order to fight in war.

Would you feel any differently if you were in charge? After all, nations need to defend themselves, right? Should a country surrender to defeat simply because not enough people volunteer to fight the enemy? Or, on rare occasions and when circumstances warrant it, should a government be able to compel its own citizens to contribute their time—and potentially their lives—to the cause? On one hand, you could argue that a nation's survival might indeed depend on the ability to mobilize a sufficient number of troops, especially during times of dire threat. On the other hand, forcing individuals to fight against their will challenges the very notion of freedom that should be the bedrock of any country's law.

The Context

Leave it to a former slave to see the clear problem with conscription. Frederick Douglass was born into slavery and escaped at the age of twenty, later becoming a famous abolitionist, using his writing and speaking skills to further the cause and raise awareness of the evil nature of slavery. In speeches and his three autobiographies, Douglass vividly detailed the brutal realities of slavery and his journey to liberation. When the conscription law was passed, he noted how ironic it was that the government was willing to classify Black people as citizens because it was politically expedient and would help swell the military's ranks. Douglass pushed back both on that idea and the concept undergirding conscription:

> What is freedom? It is the right to choose one's own employment. Certainly it means that, if it means anything. And when any individual or combination of

individuals, undertakes to decide for any man when he shall work, where he shall work, at what he shall work, and for what he shall work, he or they practically reduce him to slavery. He is a slave.

Enslaving people—citizens or otherwise—in order to provide the government with more people to fight a war is not new; the Civil War was just another link in a long chain of conscription events. Before modern professional armies created a warrior class of military elites, historical kingdoms often employed a system of conscription. For example, in the Babylonian empire, a system called *Ilkum* was used, where laborers were required to provide military service in exchange for the right to own land. Similar systems were used in Europe during the Middle Ages. The feudal system required peasants to join the military when required by either the king or the local lord. And throughout medieval Scandinavia, farmers were conscripted into coastal fleets to sail against invading hordes.

In modern times, conscription gained a toehold during the French Revolution. In 1792, the Revolutionary Wars pitted France against Great Britain, Austria, Prussia, and Russia. These external conflicts required a large military that France felt compelled to create using conscription. Compounding the problem was the internal turmoil in the country: an insurrection that August where armed revolutionaries stormed Paris to fight the monarchy; the abolition of the monarchy the following month; the execution of Louis XVI in January 1793; another revolt that June; 16,000 people being executed in a Reign of Terror; the new Republic being replaced in 1795 by the five-member governing committee called the Directory; and four years later when Napoleon Bonaparte seized power in a military coup. This internal instability led to a vulnerable position since other countries saw the weakness and wanted to take advantage, including neighboring monarchies who wanted to help put down the revolts, lest they spread to their own country. The *Levée en masse*, or mass national conscription, first began as a short-term emergency measure in 1793. In 1798, it was formalized in a law that stated, "Any Frenchman is a soldier and owes himself to the defense of the nation." All single and childless men aged 20–25 were drafted—over 2.6 million of them in the 15 years that followed.

While France was the first, they certainly weren't the last. In the US, the precedent set during the Civil War gave rise to additional rounds of conscription in succeeding military conflicts. As World War I ramped up and the US entered the conflict in April 1917, President Woodrow Wilson's administration set a target of one million enlisted volunteers to join the military and fight in the war within the first six weeks. Only 73,000 people volunteered. Consequently, Wilson decided to rely primarily on conscription, signing into law the Selective Service Act of 1917, which first required all men aged 21–30 to register for military service; this was expanded the following year, at the request of the War Department, to span ages 18–45. By the end of 1918, nearly three million men were inducted into the military. Unlike during the Civil War, there was little resistance to the draft—thanks in part to the government shutting down newspapers and other media that dissented and might encourage people to dodge the draft.

What happened during World War I became a model for World War II. President Roosevelt signed the Selective Training and Service Act in 1940, which created the first peacetime draft in the US. The 1940 law instituted conscription in peacetime, requiring the registration of all men between twenty-one and thirty-five. After Pearl Harbor was attacked, the age span was increased to ages 18–64. During the span of the war, some 49 million men were registered for potential service, with around 10 million of them being drafted into the military. Around 373,000 allegedly evaded the draft, and over 16,000 of them were thrown in prison.

Conscription continued during the Korean War, with over 1.5 million men being drafted. During the Vietnam War, 2.2 million men were drafted. And while more recent wars have not involved conscription, the opportunity still exists, as men between the ages of eighteen and twenty-five are required to register with the Selective Service System within thirty days of their eighteenth birthday. Failure to register is a felony punishable by up to five years in prison or a $250,000 fine. (In practice, no one has been prosecuted since 1986, partly due to past experience in prosecuting draft dodgers proving to be counterproductive.)

Why is it the Worst Idea?

The Draft Riot of 1863 was not an isolated event during the war between the states. Many other smaller skirmishes broke out, such as one year prior in Wisconsin when the local newspaper described how the draft commissioner, one Mr. Pors, was assaulted as he tried to do his duties:

> Mr. Pors then spoke to [the crowd] in a mild manner, requesting them to stand back a little and they could all see that the draft was conducted properly. At this

was a rush forward. Many of them were armed with
clubs, many had huge stones in their hands, and others
had various implements. The first thing done was to
demolish the draft box with a club, and they seized
hold of Mr. Pors, and rather trampled upon him, the
women vying with the men in the brutish assault.

The crowd then proceeded to hurl him down the court-house steps. Mr. Pors fled for his life as some of the rioters threw rocks at him. After he left, the group turned back to the courthouse and tore up the enrollment lists. One might look at such protests involving physical assault and consider them an egregious escalation of violence. That's a fair argument, yet it fails to contemplate that the actions of these individuals can be construed as defensive in nature. Would we really object to an African young man in the antebellum South fighting and injuring his would-be captors? In this light, the violent resistance to conscription during the Civil War (and subsequent wars) can be seen as a form of self-defense against what many perceived as an unjust and coercive act by the government—a literal attempt to enslave those drafted into combat. These individuals, whether in New York, Wisconsin, or elsewhere, were not merely reacting to the immediate threat of being drafted; they were defending their fundamental right to autonomy and self-determination. To them, conscription was akin to being forced into servitude, stripped of their freedom, and compelled to fight in a war they might not believe in or understand.

And that is why conscription is the worst—it is a sanctioned form of slavery that persists today in the form of the Selective Service System that maintains a database of potential victims. It is an involuntary servitude in which the government lays claim to the labor—and thus the very bodies—of those coerced into military involvement. (Oddly, the 13th Amendment, which was enacted after the Civil War and which prohibits involuntary servitude, does not prevent the government from continuing conscription.) By depriving people of controlling themselves and determining how they wish to spend their time and energy, it becomes *de facto* slavery; this cannot be justified simply because politicians, instead of private slaveowners, are the ones in charge. As Murray Rothbard wrote in 1973:

> If you and I and our next-door neighbor think that we need defending, we have no moral right to use coercion—the bayonet or the revolver—to force someone else to defend us. This act of conscripting is just as much a deed of unjustifiable aggression—of kidnapping and possibly murder—as the alleged aggression we are trying to guard ourselves against in the first place. If we add that the draftees owe their bodies and their lives, if necessary, to "society" or to "their country," then we must retort: who is this "society" or this "country" that is being used as a talisman to justify enslavement? It is simply all individuals in the territorial area except the youths being conscripted. "Society" and "country" are in this case mythical abstractions that are being used to cloak the naked use of coercion to promote the interests of specific individuals.

There's also an argument to be made that conscription is *worse* than what we typically call slavery. Where slavery exists (and let's be clear, any and all forms of slavery are evil), slaveowners at least have an economic interest in protecting the lives of the individuals they claim as property. Like an important tool, they want to preserve it so it can fulfill its intended purpose; and while they might mistreat a slave, they are incentivized to restrain themselves and ensure the individual remains alive and is sufficiently fed and sheltered. The government has no such incentive for the individuals it drafts into its military. Conscripts are sent into conflict that may well turn out to be more degrading and deadly than what slaves once faced, forced to give their lives in furtherance of a cause they do not believe in and did not sign up for. And those who survive these hostilities are typically tossed aside after the fact, soon ignored and forgotten after the fighting ends.

In every sense imaginable, conscription is a grave infringement on individual freedom, reducing citizens to mere tools of the state, sacrificed for political agendas they did not choose.

A World Without It

Case 5787, *United States of America vs. Robert Paul Zaugh*, went on trial on Tuesday, May 26, 1970. Zaugh, only twenty-five years old at the time, stood and faced the judge to answer charges for refusing to report for induction into the military. He was one of many draft dodgers and resisters during the Vietnam War, exploiting loopholes and deliberately pushing back on a system widely seen as unjust. Zaugh represented himself without an attorney and explained in simple terms why he was refusing to fight: because of conscription, he said, "Young people are dispossessed of their lives in this country, and that as a result we are being deprived of life, liberty, and the pursuit of happiness. I maintain that I have the right to choose my own happiness; not to have it imposed upon me from the outside." Conscription was slavery, he explained.

Zaugh was joined by tens of thousands of others who pushed back on the government's assertion that they owed a duty to render their time, energy, and their very lives in service of a war half a world away. Most notable among the resisters was world heavyweight champion Muhammad Ali. He was sentenced to prison in 1967 for resisting the draft. "Why should they ask me to put on a uniform and go 10,000 miles from home and drop bombs and bullets on brown people in Vietnam while so-called Negro people in Louisville are treated like dogs?" Ali provocatively inquired.

Draft resistance reached its peak in 1972 when there were more conscientious objectors—people refusing to participate for moral or religious reasons—than there were actual drafters. All major cities had huge backlogs of legal cases from people refusing the draft. It was a successful campaign against conscription; there were too many people to punish or send to prison, and the pushback was so widespread that President Carter later passed a general amnesty to everyone who fled abroad in defiance of the draft. The draft resistance and its widely reported controversies brought significant attention to the ethical and moral issues surrounding the Vietnam War. High-profile acts of resistance, such as burning draft cards and public refusals to serve, were covered extensively by the media. This coverage helped galvanize public opposition to the war, as people saw their fellow citizens—often young men— willing to face legal consequences rather than participate in what they viewed as an unjust conflict. The growing antiwar sentiment, fueled by draft resistance, put pressure on politicians and policymakers. As the antiwar movement gained momentum, it became a significant factor in electoral politics. Politicians, particularly those seeking re-election, had to respond to the increasing public demand to end the war.

In other words, the Vietnam War ended in large measure due to the public pushback against participation—the building opposition to conscription. If the government could not compel people to go fight, then who would? Not enough. And this is the promise of a world without conscription—an obstacle in the path of warmongering politicians who would have a hard time furthering their interventionist agenda without being able to build up the military through conscription. Reliance on an all-volunteer military helps mitigate this tendency; if the public clearly sees that a particular war is unjust, it will be hard to persuade them to go fight and potentially die. By banning conscription, we would be removing an incentive for corrupt politicians who see individuals as mere cannon fodder, like pieces in a strategy game to be moved around the board at their whim. But abolishing conscription would also be a clear repudiation of state-sanctioned slavery in all forms. It could lead to a greater awakening of individual rights and personal autonomy, representing a commitment to the idea that every person has the right to decide their own destiny, free from coercive state mandates.

Slavery can only persist if people accept their chains. In the case of human chattel slavery, the system began breaking down once slaves started rising up against their masters and fleeing bondage to seek freedom in the North. Similarly, resistance against military conscription can end unjust wars like what happened in Vietnam. After all, people with the freedom to fully control their own lives and bodies are not likely to join a conflict that is unjust and unnecessary. By rejecting conscription and standing up for individual liberty, we can ensure that the power to wage war is kept in check and that personal freedom remains paramount.

Tuttle Twins Takeaways

1. Conscription infringes on personal freedom and autonomy by forcing individuals to serve in the military against their will.

2. Many people have resisted being drafted into the military, from the Civil War to the Vietnam War, which is a reasonable act of self-defense against being compelled to fight.

3. The Selective Service System is a lingering form of potential coercion, maintaining a database of individuals for possible future conscription.

4. Abolishing conscription removes a tool that can be exploited by politicians to engage in unnecessary and unjust wars.

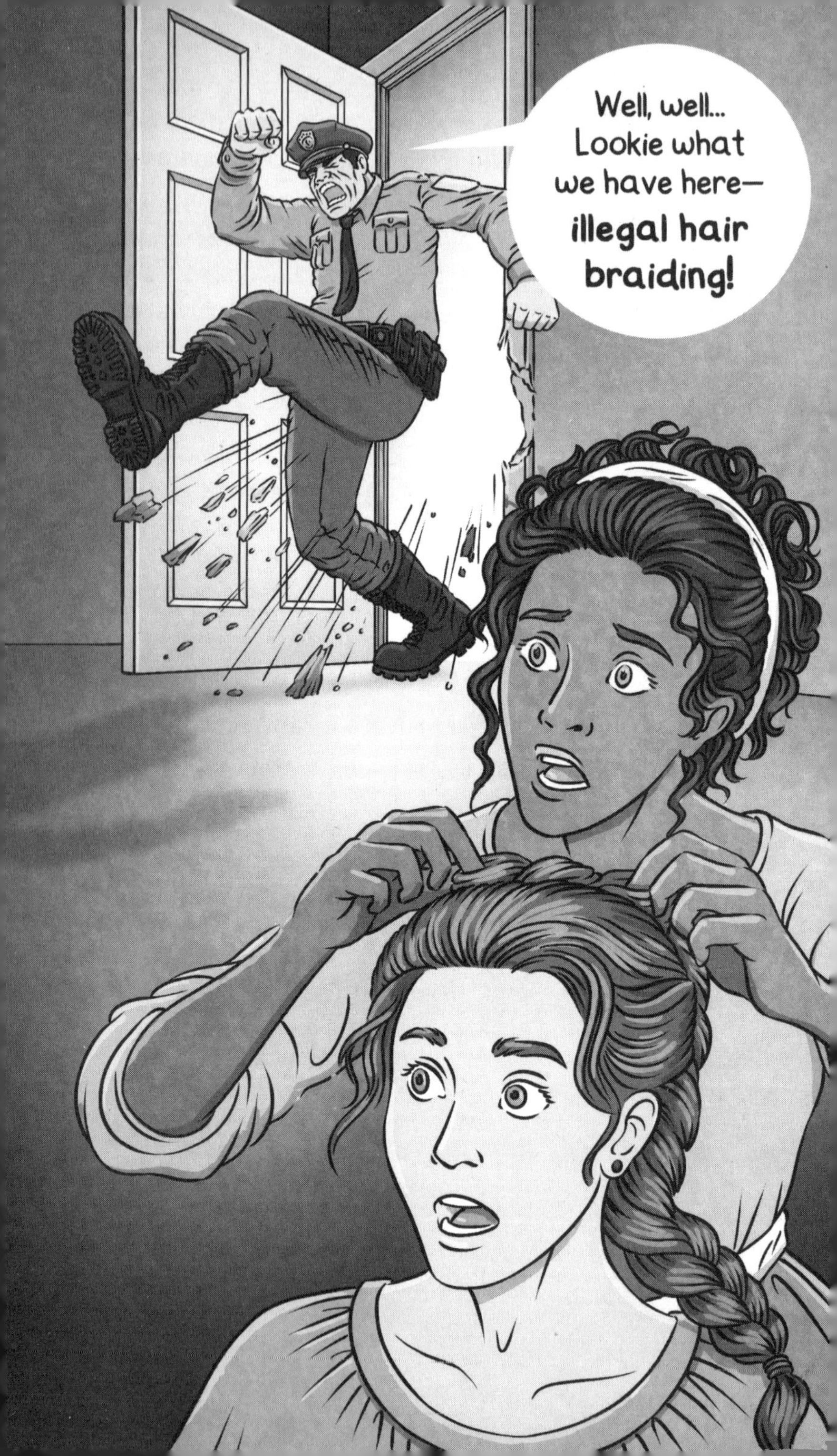
Well, well... Lookie what we have here— illegal hair braiding!

OCCUPATIONAL LICENSURE

By restricting entry into certain professions, licensure laws infringe on the fundamental right to work and pursue one's chosen career.

"Licensing restrictions are seldom designed for the benefit of consumers. More often, they are imposed for the benefit of those already in the industry, keeping out competition."

~ Thomas Sowell

The Middle Ages began after the fall of the Roman Empire in the fifth century—and for hundreds of years, Europe remained a battleground for conquest and turmoil. The Byzantine Wars, the Arab Conquests, the Viking Raids, and other invasions and wars all contributed to an unrelenting fixation on survival. But by 1000 A.D., Europe had somewhat stabilized, and conflicts no longer consumed the majority of people's attention and energy. The population increased (since far fewer people were being killed), agricultural advancements boosted food production, and people began producing and exchanging luxury items. This economic boom was the result of a merchant economy, where people could specialize in particular crafts and offer their services in exchange for essentials that they needed to live and enjoy their lives.

Artisans and craftsmen began forming associations within their industries to protect their economic interests. These guilds, as they came to be known, enabled members to provide mutual aid to one another while regulating how their profession would operate and combining their political power to defend their rights against external threats from people not in the guild. As the population grew and the size of towns and cities increased in the eleventh and twelfth centuries, guilds began seeking formal recognition from the government. They were granted charters that recognized their existence and allowed them to self-regulate their own trades. With that authority, guilds established strict rules and standards to ensure the quality (and high price) of their goods and services. They were able to control labor by dictating who could join the guild and under what terms people could work in their profession; this regulated the competition and allowed them to maintain high prices.

For example, the Hanseatic League was a powerful confederation of merchant guilds and market towns in Northwestern and Central Europe, formed in the late twelfth century and lasting until the seventeenth century. Originating in the city of Lübeck, the League grew to encompass over 200 towns across modern-day Germany, Poland, the Baltic states, and Scandinavia. It facilitated trade by establishing a network of mutually supportive cities that ensured safe passage and economic privileges for its members. The League dominated maritime trade in the North and Baltic Seas and wielded significant political influence, negotiating treaties, and even waging wars to protect its interests. But guilds such as these declined in the shadow of powerful nation-states that created trade routes that challenged the guilds' stranglehold on commerce. The rise of factories and the advent of mass production during the Industrial Revolution transformed industries that had long been dominated by small-scale artisans. The guilds, with their traditions and monopolies, were ill-suited to this new era of capitalism.

So the monopolies were gradually removed and trade was liberalized. But the artisans, merchants, and professional practitioners still wanted to regulate their professions, reduce competition, and reward themselves with high prices. Within the protection of a guild, how could they accomplish these goals?

The Context

John Brinkley arrived in Chicago in the spring of 1908 after spending a year in Tennessee apprenticed to a medical miracle worker who used various tonics to help men cure their impotence. Chicago was home to multiple medical schools, each teaching a different approach to medicine—allopathic, homeopathic, osteopathic, etc. He ultimately decided on the Bennett Eclectic Medical College, an unaccredited school that focused primarily on herbal remedies. He borrowed the $25 fee he needed to enter the school and began his studies. He returned home three years later, failing to complete the curriculum and pay the tuition he owed. Now in St. Louis, Missouri, Brinkley wanted to resume his studies, but the college he had attended refused to forward his school records to any of the new schools he was pursuing since he had not paid them the tuition they were due. Instead, he bought a medical certificate from the Kansas City Eclectic Medical University, a business that sold illegitimate diplomas and degrees for a simple fee.

Over the next several years, Brinkley moved from town to town as he pursued his ill-gotten trade. He built a small fortune providing the same services in which he had apprenticed: a cure-all for impotence. His approach included more than mere tonics; Brinkley would transplant live goat testicles into humans. Soon after, the wife of his first goat gland transplant patient gave birth to a baby boy, prompting Brinkley to promote goat glands as a cure for twenty-seven ailments, including dementia and even flatulence. Along the way, critics argued against his methods, and many of his patients died, forcing the medical board in Kansas, where he had moved, to hold a formal hearing to determine whether he should be barred from being a doctor. At that point, over forty of Brinkley's patients had died, many of whom were not sick when arriving at his clinic; it is not known how many more became sick or later died elsewhere. With a mountain of evidence working against him, the Kansas Medical Board stripped Brinkley of his medical license, stating that he "has performed an organized charlatanism."

This example, one of countless others, demonstrates the evolution from guilds into their modern form: occupational licensing boards. Though different in form and style, these committees are typically comprised of people from the profession who are given the power by the government to punish their peers and even deny them from operating in the profession. Governments across America had, by Brinkley's time, created licensure requirements stipulating that doctors would be required to meet certain criteria, pay a fee, and pass an approved exam in order to legally work. And by requiring this government permission slip, boards like the one Brinkley faced were empowered to shut someone down by revoking that license, without which one's work is not legal. The power to license a profession is the power to destroy one's livelihood.

Frank Dent faced a similar situation. He was a practicing physician who was denied his right to work under a new state law that required a medical license. He had been practicing medicine for years, but the new law in his state, West Virginia, demanded proof of adequate medical education and a license. Dent decided to sue, arguing that these requirements infringed on his right to practice in his profession. The case made it all the way to the US Supreme Court and attracted national attention. In the 1888 ruling on *Dent v. West Virginia*, the Court upheld the state's right to require licenses for professions like medicine, asserting that they had the quantity to grant licenses to protect the health, welfare, and safety of their citizens.

One might reasonably argue that a licensure scheme for doctors is appropriate, given the risks involved in operating on humans and prescribing medicines. When one's life is on the line, it's generally a good idea to have some sort of process in place to ensure the doctor is well trained and operating in the patient's best interest; keeping charlatans like Brinkley away from patients is obviously a good thing. But just like the medieval guilds and their breadth across industries, modern occupation licensure did not restrict itself to the medical field. Empowered by the 1888 ruling and its broad interpretation of state power, licensure requirements quickly expanded to other professions, egged on by the professionals themselves, who wanted the gatekeeping and protectionism that guilds once afforded. As economist Milton Friedman noted in 1945, "In all professions, there has developed in the last few years an aristocratic, or at least a restrictive movement which, in a sense, is reminiscent of the medieval guilds." By the mid-1900s, licensure had grown to cover professions like engineering, law, accounting, and more, involving about five percent of the entire US workforce. Within three decades, the number of licensed professions skyrocketed, now covering more than 25 percent of the economy; two-thirds of this expansion is due to the increase in the number of occupations for which a license is now required. Consider this partial list of professions for which varying states require a license:

- Animal breeders

- Barbers

- Cat groomers

- Cosmetologists

- Elevator operators

- Florists

- Interior designers

- Makeup artists

- Plumbers

- Sheep dealers

- Tour or travel guides

- Upholsterers

Why is it the Worst Idea?

Mats Järlström is a Swedish engineer living in Oregon. One day, his wife received a ticket in the mail after she was captured on camera crossing into an intersection after the traffic light had turned red. In response, Järlström created and proposed a new mathematical formula for the traffic cameras to use, which would account for cars slowing down before changing a yellow light to red. "I'm an excellent engineer," he told the Oregon State Board of Examiners for Engineering and Land Surveying.

That statement led the board to impose a $500 fine on him following a two-year investigation. Why? He hadn't done anything inherently wrong; there was no victim of his math formula on paper. The board punished him for calling himself an engineer without their permission. Here is their ruling:

> Järlström applied special knowledge of the mathematical, physical and engineering sciences to such creative work as investigation, evaluation and design in connection with public equipment, processes and works. Järlström thereby engaged in the practice of engineering.

Good thing neither Nikola Tesla nor Leonardo da Vinci lived in Oregon; otherwise, they might have been fined for having the audacity to consider themselves engineers without first obtaining the blessing of the bureaucracy. Stories such as Järlström's are unfortunately abundant, featuring overbearing regulatory burdens on peaceful, hardworking people. Consider Jestina Clayton, a woman from Sierra Leone who had been taught traditional African hair braiding since she was a young child. Later in life, she relocated to Utah and discovered a number of white families who had adopted Black children but who didn't know how to braid their hair. Clayton decided to offer her services to these families as a side hustle and began advertising her services online. A licensed cosmetologist in the state saw her ad and sent her this email: "It is illegal in the state of Utah to do any form of [braiding] without a valid cosmetology license. Please delete your ad, or you will be reported." This person had the law on their side; licensure laws in Utah at the time stated that a person could not manipulate hair in any way, including simply braiding it, for compensation unless they obtained a license that required 2,000 hours—a full year, full time—of government-mandated cosmetology training. The kicker? Cosmetology schools didn't even teach African hair braiding, and Clayton had substantially more practical experience than any of the students or teachers at these schools. In response to the threat, Clayton shut down her business.

Imagine yourself in one of these situations. You have knowledge, experience, and an economic opportunity to offer your services to others. You are competent and qualified, and your services are in demand. Then someone in your industry, empowered by the law, decides to shut you down because they see you as inferior competition and a threat to the regulatory fiefdom they've built. No one was harmed; there were no actual complaints. They simply wanted to use the protectionist law to keep you out so that they could benefit themselves. Occupational licensure is one of the worst ideas ever because the government presumes to ban you from your desired profession without first obtaining their permission slip. These laws typically make you jump over unnecessary hurdles, such as attending school to learn things not relevant to your particular niche. Licensure is, to put it plainly, the violation of a person's right to work.

That right has not been adequately protected. While the courts have generally deferred to government agencies and their power to broadly regulate professions for reasons of "public health and safety," there have been a few instances of judicial recognition of the right to work. Clayton's story didn't end with the shuttering of her business; she teamed up with the Institute for Justice to sue the government in federal court, asserting her right to work. And the judge, in her case, agreed: "The right to work for a living in the common occupations of the community is of the very essence of the personal freedom and opportunity that the Constitution was designed to protect." This echoed a 1923 US Supreme Court ruling in which the majority opinion stated that the Due Process Clause of the US Constitution "without doubt... denotes the right of the individual... to engage in any of the common occupations of life."

These few, occasional judicial recognitions are in the minority; across the country, courts have permitted the pervasive influence of occupational licensure, which stifles innovation and economic growth. Licensure creates an artificial barrier to entry, often necessitating costly and time-consuming compliance that is disproportionate to the skills required for the job. And who gets put in charge? All too often, the regulatory boards that oversee each profession are largely composed of people *within* that profession who have a personal interest in excluding others so as to not face much competition, lowering their prices and making their life difficult. These boards can impose waiting periods and fees to make entry more difficult and keep out-of-state practitioners from working in their state. They can sometimes alter exam pass rates, making it more difficult to achieve the necessary score to obtain a license. And they sometimes can control the accreditation of the training schools and the number of openings available. Like the guilds long before them, they are granted legal power to protect their profession from external threats, including competition.

All of this is at the expense of individuals like Järlström and Clayton. Occupational licensure is the worst idea because it not only violates free market principles but also infringes upon the fundamental right to work. By imposing arbitrary barriers, it suppresses innovation, entrepreneurship, and personal initiative. It empowers a select few to control the fate of many, fostering an environment of protectionism and cronyism that benefits established players while marginalizing new entrants. Ultimately, these laws do more harm than good, stifling economic growth, increasing costs for consumers, and perpetuating inequality.

A World Without It

Without occupational licensure—without the government blessing certain workers with its stamp of approval—would society descend into chaos? Would unqualified individuals roam around the marketplace, foisting their dangerous services onto an unsuspecting public? Hardly. A world without government-mandated occupational licensure doesn't mean a world without standards or safety measures. In fact, removing these artificial barriers could lead to more innovation, increased economic opportunities, and potentially even *better* consumer protection.

Under the current regime, people operate under the basic assumption that someone with a license has met certain minimum standards required by the government in order to be considered competent and qualified to work in that profession. This low-information approach involves a mere permission slip to discern whether someone would be a good worker, as if all architects, barbers, or cosmetologists with such licenses have similar capabilities, quality, and standard of service. Abolishing licensure would incentivize people to discard these poor criteria in favor of market-driven solutions for ensuring quality and safety. Just as we rely on customer reviews and ratings when shopping on Amazon or choosing a restaurant, consumers would turn to similar systems to evaluate professionals and service providers. These peer-driven feedback mechanisms would become crucial in helping people make informed decisions about whom to trust with their health, home repairs, or legal matters. College students can use services like Rate My Professor to gather feedback on teachers in order to determine which class to take. Imagine that approach, but for every profession, where there are websites to utilize to determine which person to hire for your job. Perhaps you could access a plumber's entire work history, complete with detailed customer reviews, photos of completed jobs, and even video testimonials. You could see how they've handled complex problems, their punctuality record, and how they've resolved any customer complaints. This level of transparency would incentivize professionals to maintain high standards and provide excellent service, as their livelihood would depend directly on their reputation.

This approach solicits the wisdom of the crowd; a thousand reviews from others, even if some are fake or malicious, are superior to the arbitrary whims of licensing boards and bureaucrats. Beyond review websites, private certifications could add more wisdom from the crowds, with professional associations and independent organizations offering voluntary certifications for workers to obtain, which could provide consumers with information about a person's qualifications. Insurance companies would play a significant role in this new landscape, especially for higher-risk professions. They might require certain qualifications or ongoing education before providing malpractice coverage, creating a natural incentive for professionals to maintain high standards. This approach could be more flexible and responsive to new developments in various fields than the often slow-to-change government licensing boards.

A world without licensure would also focus on education where it matters. Instead of compelling the Jestina Claytons of the world to navigate 2,000 hours of schooling that is not relevant to her chosen niche, schools would be incentivized to teach practical, valuable skills that truly prepare students for their chosen niches. We would also see a resurgence of apprenticeship models, where aspiring professionals learn through hands-on experience under the guidance of seasoned experts.

The government does a poor job of keeping people safe. Police don't prevent crime—they show up after the fact to write a report and potentially investigate. Food safety laws don't stop some commercial kitchens from selling tainted food. The FDA's drug approval process hasn't stopped dangerous drugs from entering the market, killing many. Just like the TSA is "security theater," creating the *appearance* of safety without actually ensuring it, licensure laws offer "safety theater" where consumers might *feel* safe. But handing out government permission slips is not a reliable way to actually attest to the competence, safety, and quality of work of a particular person. Abolishing licensure in favor of some of the market-based approaches described here would lead to greater consumer safety, and bad actors could still be prosecuted and prohibited from future work in their chosen profession due to laws against fraud, negligence, and malpractice that generally apply to everyone, regardless of their industry. The key difference is that these protections would be reactive rather than preemptive, punishing bad actors rather than creating barriers for everyone.

Occupational licensure is a relic of an outdated system that stifles innovation, limits economic opportunities, and provides a false sense of security. By embracing market-driven solutions and empowering consumers with information, we can create a more dynamic, efficient, and truly safe marketplace. The right to work is fundamental to human liberty and prosperity. It's time we recognize that government permission slips do more harm than good and that individuals, not bureaucrats, are best equipped to make decisions about their lives and livelihoods. In a world of increasing connectivity and information sharing, we have better tools than ever to ensure quality and safety without resorting to heavy-handed government intervention.

Tuttle Twins Takeaways

1. Occupational licensure is a modern form of medieval guilds, restricting who can work in certain professions.

2. These laws often create unnecessary barriers, especially for low-income individuals and entrepreneurs.

3. The stated purpose of licensure is public safety, but it often fails to achieve this goal effectively. It provides a false sense of security rather than actual consumer protection.

4. Licensure violates the fundamental right to work and pursue a chosen profession.

5. Alternative, market-based solutions can provide better consumer protection.

EMINENT DOMAIN

When the state claims the ability to take your property without your consent, do you actually own it?

"Even the most narrowly construed eminent-domain power violates individual rights. Either a person owns his legitimately acquired property or he does not."

~ Sheldon Richman

The Colorado River had long flowed from the Rocky Mountains to the Gulf of California, along its 1,450-mile course. The Imperial Valley in California is fertile ground for growing a variety of crops, but the water supplied by the river was unpredictable; floods would occur in the spring, devastating surrounding farmlands, and the summer would be quite dry. By the 1920s, the damage from flooding had attracted so much attention that leaders began putting their heads together on a way to control the path—and output—of the lower Colorado. Building a dam would be an essential element in the plan to harness the vast amount of water streaming down the river—and doing so would create an added benefit of providing much-needed electricity to western states.

Congress took up consideration of the Boulder Canyon Project Act in 1928—a bill that authorized the construction of the Hoover Dam. Over $165 million was appropriated for construction (over $3 billion in today's dollars), and the Act took effect following ratification of the Colorado River Compact by six of the seven states of the Colorado River Basin. The project first required diverting the river's water, which was accomplished by drilling four large tunnels, each 50 feet wide, through the solid rock walls of Black Canyon. Sixteen thousand people worked on the project, with around 3,500 employed at any given time; the dangerous work was arduous, killing nearly a hundred men. But none of the work would have been possible without the power of eminent domain.

The town of St. Thomas, Nevada, was home to nearly 500 residents at its peak. Established in 1865 as a Mormon settlement, the town was forced to terminate when the

Boulder Canyon Project began; while the new dam would bring benefits to people across the American Southwest, the people of St. Thomas were forced to find new homes because theirs would soon be underwater. The dam's construction would create a reservoir, Lake Mead, that soon submerged St. Thomas. Its residents were bought out as a result of the government empowering itself under the new Act "to acquire by proceedings in eminent domain, or otherwise all lands, rights-of-way, and other property necessary" to build the dam. In the throes of the Great Depression, most of the tenants were eager to cash out and relocate. Wayne Bunker and his family were one of the last to leave. Later in life, he said that "The government had an appraiser, the residents had an appraiser and a third appraiser was brought in. The government was fair. You have to remember, this was the Great Depression, and money was tight. People were happy to get cash they could invest in other land and businesses." Using eminent domain, the government purchased not only the land necessary for the project but also the water rights of people who had laid claim to some of the river's flow. The dam was, in the eyes of President Hoover, "the greatest engineering work of its character ever attempted by the hand of man."

While many saw this as a necessary sacrifice for the greater good of the region, it raises important questions about the power of government to forcibly displace people from their homes and communities. Because of economic conditions and cultural attitudes, it appears that no one in St. Thomas outright objected to the acquisition of their property by the federal government. But imagine if someone had resisted—one family in St. Thomas standing their ground, refusing to sell their property regardless of the price offered. Had this happened, the government would have ultimately resorted to force to remove them from their property. This could have involved legal action, fines, and potentially even physical removal by law enforcement. The family's deep connection to their home, their land, and their community would have been disregarded in favor of the government's plans. Considering this circumstance, it reveals that eminent domain is not a voluntary transaction between a willing buyer and seller but a coercive act backed by the threat of government force.

The Context

Hugo Grotius, a Dutch statesman, wrote *On the Law of War and Peace* in 1625 in an attempt to lay the groundwork for a universal code of conduct in international relations. His focus was primarily on war and foreign policy, though the book argued for the existence and use of a variety of other governmental powers. Grotius wrote of *dominium eminens*, or supreme lordship, and said:

> The property of subjects is under the eminent domain of the state, so that the state or he who acts for it may use and even alienate and destroy such property, not only in the case of extreme necessity, in which even private persons have a right over the property of others, but for ends of public utility, to which ends those who founded civil society must be supposed to have intended that private ends should give way. But it is to be added that when this is done the state is bound to make good the loss to those who lose their property.

From this work derives the term eminent domain—the purported authority of the state, or its functionaries, to take property from people when "public utility" demands it. To the greater good, these property owners "should give way," hoping to receive sufficient compensation from the good graces of those in power. Building on Grotius' legal analysis, courts in the centuries since have all agreed, recognizing eminent domain as an inherent power of a sovereign state to lord over its subjects. In *Boom Co. v. Patterson*, an 1879 ruling by the US Supreme Court said that the power "appertains to every independent government. It requires no constitutional recognition; it is an attribute of sovereignty." Four years prior, in *Kohl v. United States*, the Court called eminent domain "essential to [the government's] independent existence and perpetuity." And a century before that, despite calling it a "despotic power," the Court affirmed in the 1795 case *Vanhorne's Lessee v. Dorrance* that "the existence of such power is necessary; government could not subsist without it."

Grotius' stipulation that the state must "make good the loss to those who lose their property" found its way not into the original Constitution but rather the Fifth Amendment as part of the later-passed Bill of Rights. It reads, in part, "…nor shall private property be taken for public use, without just compensation." This provision did not create the federal government's authority to take property—it simply limited it by requiring that when property is taken for public use, the original owner must be compensated. Of course, actual compensation is hard to determine. Assessors can review nearby and comparable properties to determine the market rate for a property, and the government will deem this just compensation. But for the person living in their childhood home, full of decades of memories, the value is worth more than others might be willing to pay. Yet this does not matter for the government; you receive what it is willing to give.

Early uses of eminent domain in America were primarily limited to true public uses, such as roads, bridges, parks, and public buildings. The power first expanded when the government authorized private companies, such as those building railroads, to take property in order to lay down their tracks and utilities. At least in these cases, though private companies, they were required as a condition of using eminent domain to provide the public equal access to the rail lines and utilities. Things changed drastically in 1954 with the case *Berman v. Parker*, when the US Supreme Court expanded the definition of what might be considered "public use" for eminent domain purposes. The Court said in this case that "urban renewal"—government projects aimed at renewing urban districts, allegedly to clear slums and improve deteriorating areas—can qualify for taking one's property. Now "public use" meant "public purpose," greatly expanding the government's opportunity for eminent domain by creating a financial incentive for private developers to persuade politicians that a particular area was blighted and required urban renewal. Governments began expanding their definitions of what constitutes blight, enabling them to condemn perfectly fine properties—businesses, homes, and more—in order for private developers to take control and build something new, ostensibly to increase tax revenue for the municipality by having the land turned into a more productive purpose.

Why is it the Worst Idea?

Susette Kelo purchased a small Victorian cottage in the Fort Trumbull neighborhood of New London, Connecticut, in 1997. The house, built in 1893, had fallen into disrepair, but Kelo saw its potential. She lovingly restored the home, painting it a soft pink color that would later become iconic in the legal battle that followed. For Kelo, a nurse and lifelong resident of the area, this modest house represented the American Dream of homeownership and a fresh start after a divorce. The Fort Trumbull neighborhood, while not affluent, was a tight-knit community where many residents had lived for decades. Kelo's home overlooked the Thames River, offering picturesque views that she treasured. However, unbeknownst to her at the time of purchase, powerful forces were already at work that would threaten her newfound haven.

In 1998, pharmaceutical giant Pfizer announced plans to build a major research facility adjacent to Fort Trumbull. Sensing an opportunity for economic development, the city of New London crafted an ambitious plan to redevelop the area. This plan included a hotel, office spaces, and new housing that would complement the Pfizer complex. The catch? The city would need to acquire all the property in a 90-acre area of Fort Trumbull, including Kelo's home and those of her neighbors. When Kelo and other homeowners refused to sell, the city resorted to the power of eminent domain—and because of the *Berman* decision, the city could now take the property to give to a private developer, under the guise of urban renewal instead of there being a true "public use." New London officials argued that the economic benefits to the community constituted a public use in an attempt to justify their taking of these homes.

Kelo, along with several neighboring property owners, decided to fight back. They filed a lawsuit challenging the city's use of eminent domain, arguing that economic development did not qualify as a public use. The case, *Kelo v. City of New London*, was eventually heard by the Connecticut Supreme Court, which upheld all the government's seizures of Kelo's home and those of her neighbors in a 4–3 decision. The case was appealed to the US Supreme Court, which agreed to take it up. After hearing arguments from both sides, the nation's top court ruled 5–4 in favor of the city. Kelo and the other plaintiffs had no further options to pursue; lacking other means of legal redress, they were compelled to move out. In ruling against Kelo, the Court echoed the *Berman* case half a century prior: "The concept of the public welfare is broad and inclusive… The values it represents are spiritual as well as physical, aesthetic as well as monetary."

As Kelo's case makes clear, eminent domain is a dangerous tool that threatens the very foundation of private property rights. Imagine working hard to buy your dream home, pouring your heart and savings into fixing it up, only to have the government swoop in and take it away because some corporation wants to build a mall there. That's not just unfair—it's a complete betrayal of the American Dream. Eminent domain gives the government way too much power to interfere with our affairs. It's like giving a bully your lunch money and hoping they'll use it to buy everyone ice cream. Sure, they might claim it's for the "greater good," but who decides what that means? Usually, it's politicians and their wealthy buddies (collectively, the lunchtime bullies) who stand to profit. Meanwhile, regular folks like Kelo get kicked out of their homes and communities. It's important to understand that this isn't just about buildings—it's about people's memories, their sense of belonging, and their right to feel secure in their own homes. When the government can take your property on a whim, it erodes our freedom and turns us into renters on our own land. That's not the kind of country our founders envisioned, and it's definitely not the kind of future we should accept for ourselves.

And lest you think that eminent domain pertains only to real property—land and buildings—it should be noted that governments can also take *personal* property. Personal property is something not permanently attached to land, whether tangible (physical in nature, like a car or computer) or intangible (for example, a trademark or copyright). For example, when the Oakland Raiders were contemplating a move to Los Angeles in 1982, the city of Oakland sought to use eminent domain in order to take ownership of the franchise! In the proceeding court battle, the California Supreme Court agreed that the taking of intangible property is authorized by eminent domain and that the forcible taking of a sports franchise can be considered for "public use" under the legal definition. Two years later, when the Baltimore Colts were planning a relocation to Indianapolis, they learned from the Raiders' mistake of getting trapped in court battles after eminent domain had already begun. When whispers emerged that Maryland was thinking about using eminent domain to seize the franchise, the team moved their operations in the middle of the night—with moving vans pulling out of their facilities under the cover of darkness. No longer in Maryland's jurisdiction, the team was safe from the state's eminent domain desires.

Not only is eminent domain horrible because the government takes your property to use for its own purposes or to hand out to another, but it's also awful because things sometimes don't even work out as intended, leading to a painful and purposeless loss on the part of the previous property owner. This was Kelo's case; the redevelopment of New London was a failure, and despite spending tens of millions of taxpayers' hard-earned dollars on the effort, with Pfizer soon abandoning their interest in the location, the land where Kelo and her neighbors previously resided lay totally bare for nearly two decades, home only to some feral cats and weeds. Finally, eighteen years after the Supreme Court case concluded, New London sold the property to a private developer to build apartments. Kelo and her neighboring homeowners were evicted, their homes razed to the ground, to make way—nearly two decades later—for... different homes.

A World Without It

Sarah Chen stood on the porch of her family's century-old farmhouse, gazing out at the fields where generations of her ancestors had tilled the soil. A developer had approached her last year with plans for a sprawling shopping complex and offered to buy her land. Sarah declined, cherishing her heritage and the quiet country life. In a world without eminent domain, that was the end of the story. The developer simply moved on, seeking willing sellers elsewhere for their project. As she sipped her morning coffee, Sarah reflected on how different things could have been. In the past, she had heard stories of families being forced off their land for "progress" or to make way for "public use," but those days were long gone. Now, her decision to keep her farm was respected and legally protected—and the Chen family legacy would continue for years to come.

Down the road, Sarah's neighbor Tom had decided to sell his property to the same developer. It was his choice, and he got a fair price that allowed him to retire comfortably. The resulting shopping center, built adjacent to Sarah's farm, had a unique charm and rustic theme to blend into its surrounding environment. Visitors often commented on how the old farmhouse added character to the area, a living testament to the region's agricultural roots amid the modern shops. In town, Main Street had become a vibrant mix of old and new, with historic buildings standing proudly next to contemporary structures. Sarah's friend Maria owned a small bookstore in that town, housed in a building that had been in her family for three generations. In the past, such a prime location might have been targeted for redevelopment, with Maria being forced out in the name of economic progress. But now, Maria's store still remains a beloved local landmark, its historical façade adding to the street's appeal and drawing in curious tourists.

As Sarah drove into town for her weekly shopping, she noticed how the community had grown and changed over the years yet retained its essential character. New businesses and homes had sprung up, but always through voluntary transactions. The result was a town that felt organic and alive, shaped by the collective decisions of its property-owning residents rather than the sweeping plans of government bureaucrats and their tax-hungry plots.

This is the vision of a world without eminent domain—one where property rights are given more than lip service, but serve as the very foundation for our interactions with one another. In this environment, we would recognize—and the law would protect—the fact that property is merely an extension of our time and energy. Like the money in our bank account, it represents past labor and value we've created, stored up in an asset that was exchanged for all that hard work. Society would recognize that to steal someone's property—even if they are provided compensation—is to steal from them directly. Would it be any better if a robber compensated you for stealing your treasured family photo album by giving you what he feels it's worth—the value of the binder and papers inside it? Obviously not; this is still theft. And worse, the compensation nowhere approaches the actual value you assign to the photo album—far more than the mere paper upon which your memories are photographically printed.

The state claims that it is sovereign, and judges across the land argue that eminent domain is an "inherent" aspect of sovereignty. But this is wrong. We, the people, are sovereign; individuals have rights, not governments. Property owners are not subjects of the king, possessing their land only with his good graces. We have natural rights—including property rights—and form governments to *secure* them. The state does not magically have inherent powers; its only just powers are those which we individuals possess and then delegate to it in order to secure our rights. And because no one has the right to take another's property, such a right cannot be exercised on behalf of the people by the government itself. Eminent domain is therefore an abuse of authority and a violation of one's rights.

The absence of eminent domain would require developers and city planners to have to work around existing properties rather than simply bulldozing them. We might see more creative architecture, better integration of old and new structures, and infrastructure solutions that truly serve the community's needs without trampling on individual rights. It would also force governments to be more accountable—instead of relying on the easy but unjust option of forcing people out, they'd have to negotiate in good faith, offer high enough prices to get people to sell, or find alternative solutions. This would naturally limit government overreach and encourage more respect for the rights of existing property owners.

Eminent domain represents a fundamental violation of our most basic rights. It's a relic of an era when kings claimed ownership over all land and subjects, not a policy befitting a free society. By allowing government to forcibly seize private property, we open the door to abuse, corruption, and the erosion of individual liberty. The Kelo case demonstrated how this power can be weaponized to benefit powerful corporations at the expense of ordinary citizens. But even when used for ostensibly public purposes, such as a large dam, eminent domain remains a coercive tool that undermines the very foundation of property rights. It turns homeowners into mere tenants, subject to eviction whenever the state deems it necessary. A truly free and just society must reject this notion entirely.

Tuttle Twins Takeaways

1. Eminent domain fundamentally violates individual property rights, prioritizing state or corporate interests over one's property rights.

2. Various court rulings have expanded the scope of eminent domain, often under dubious interpretations of "public use," leading to misuse and abuse of power.

3. Eminent domain can be abused to benefit private interests while claiming it's for the "public good," leading to corruption and cronyism.

4. The concept of eminent domain is rooted in an outdated view of government as sovereign rather than citizens as the true sovereigns.

5. Abolishing eminent domain would force governments and developers to negotiate fairly and find creative solutions rather than resorting to force.

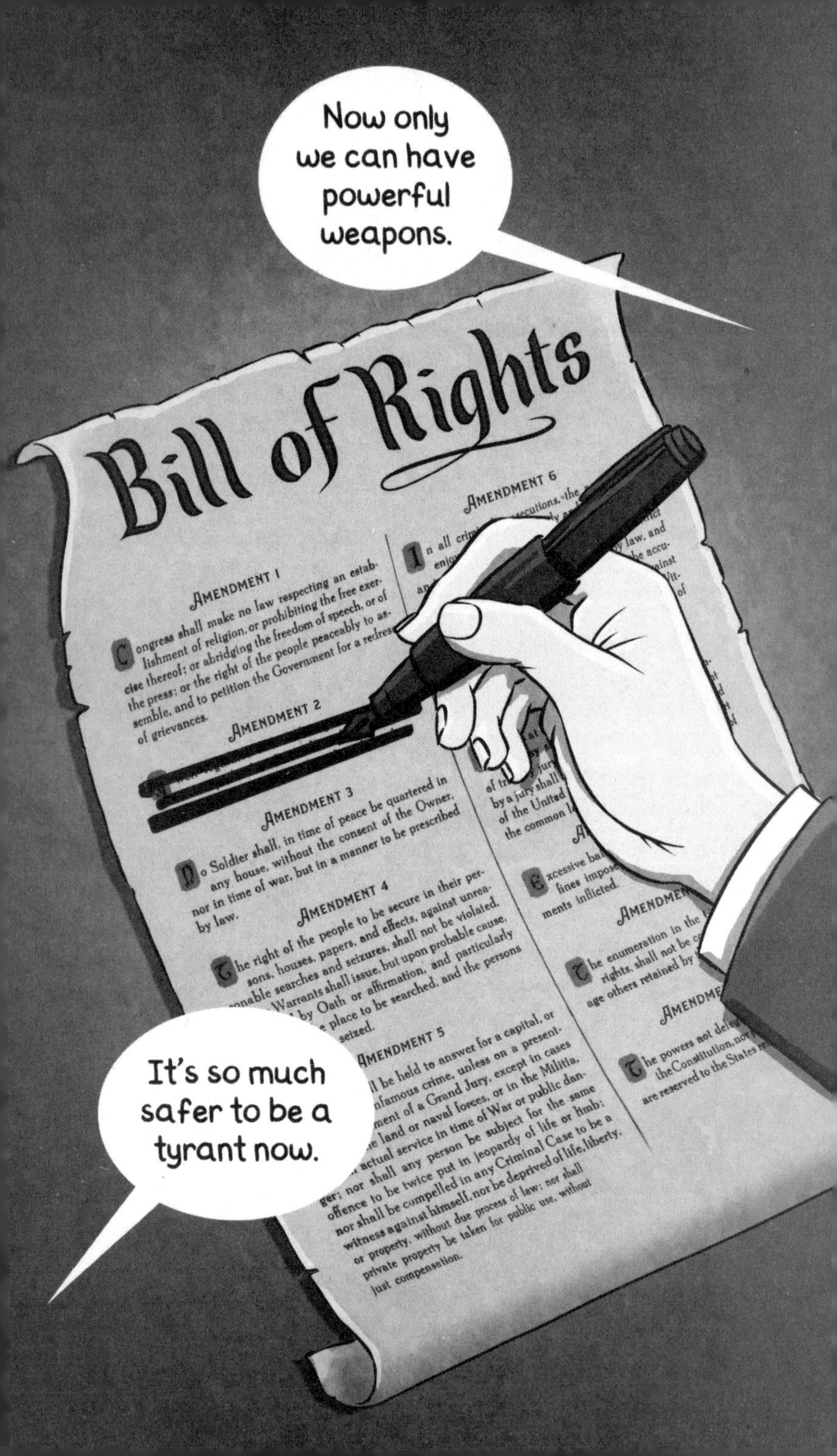

GUN
CONTROL

The inherent right to defend yourself—
whether from other individuals or your own
oppressive government—means that legal
attempts to restrict this right are invalid.

" No man has the power to
get between a human being
and their God-given right
to protect themselves and
their family."

~ Ted Nugent

On April 20, 1999, Columbine High School in Littleton, Colorado, became the site of a devastating mass shooting carried out by students Eric Harris and Dylan Klebold. The two heavily armed teenagers planned and executed an attack that began with the detonation of bombs in the school cafeteria, which failed to explode. They then proceeded to open fire on their classmates and teachers, killing twelve students and one teacher, and injuring twenty-four others before taking their own lives. The attack lasted approximately 49 minutes. A few years later, another deadly mass murder occurred at the Virginia Tech campus in Blacksburg, Virginia. Seung-Hui Cho, a twenty-three-year-old student at the university, carried out the attack in two separate incidents. The first occurred in a dormitory, where he killed two students. Two hours later, Cho entered Norris Hall, a classroom building, and began shooting, killing thirty more people and injuring seventeen others before taking his own life. A few years after that, Sandy Hook Elementary School in Newtown, Connecticut, became home to a mass shooting as well. Adam Lanza, a twenty-year-old man, began his rampage by killing his mother at their home before driving to the school. Armed with a semi-automatic rifle, he forced his way into the building and went on a shooting spree, killing twenty first-grade children and six adult staff members within minutes. The attack ended when Lanza took his own life as first responders arrived on the scene.

The day after this latter shooting, Shannon Watts, a stay-at-home mom of five kids, was still processing her emotions. "I was crying," she told a reporter. "I was glued to my television. I just was in disbelief that twenty children and six educators could be slaughtered in the sanctity of an American elementary school." She quickly decided to start a Facebook group to unite women against gun manufacturers and supporters, inspired by the way Mothers Against Drunk Driving took on the alcohol industry in the 1980s. Momentum quickly grew as volunteers from around the country reached out to inquire about starting up chapters in their own communities. The organization, Moms Demand Action for Gun Sense in America, now boasts millions of supporters and has morphed into the nation's leading gun control advocacy group, Everytown for Gun Safety. Watts and the millions of supporters behind her cause have spent their political efforts focused on securing stronger laws against gun ownership and use, fighting pro-gun organizations like the National Rifle Association along the way. They oppose laws that allow people to carry a firearm without a government permission slip, or that allow people to purchase so-called "assault weapons" like an AR-15, or that allow teachers on school campuses to be armed to defend themselves and their students. And they promote laws that require government tracking of all gun purchases, mandatory background checks for anyone who wishes to exercise their right to own and bear arms, and that allow people's guns to be taken if others perceive them to be some kind of threat.

Proponents of gun control laws believe that fewer guns will mean more safety—and that government prohibitions on one's ability to purchase and carry firearms will actually work. They argue that easy access to firearms increases the likelihood of gun-related deaths, whether through accidents, impulsive acts of violence, or mass shootings. Gun control advocates often point to statistics showing lower rates of gun violence in countries with stricter firearm regulations (countries that do not have the equivalent of the Second Amendment protecting a person's right to own and carry firearms). And in support of these gun control measures, they often cite public opinion polls showing that most people support various gun control measures, arguing that such policies reflect the will of the people and are necessary for public safety. Though well-intentioned—who doesn't want people to be safe and for mass shootings to stop?—the efforts of gun control advocates are counterproductive and problematic. Let's explore why.

The Context

King Edward II issued a proclamation on April 28, 1326, "prohibiting any one going armed without his license, except the keepers of his peace, sheriffs, and other ministers." Those who broke this rule were to be taken by the sheriff and "delivered to the nearest gallows" to be hanged. Similar restrictions imposed by the Crown previously and before were more lenient, only punishing the gun-wielding person with seizure of their firearm and imprisonment. In 1328, the Statute of Northampton was enacted into law, stipulating that no one in Britain's vast jurisdiction was allowed to "go nor ride armed by night nor by day." This law was enforced for centuries, even finding its way into the colonies and post-constitutional law in several states. Massachusetts, for example, affirmed this principle in state law by saying that officials could detain and arrest "rioters, disturbers, or breakers of the peace, and such as shall ride or go armed offensively, to the fear or terror of the good citizens of this Commonwealth."

Perhaps you astutely noted the difference, though. Whereas the Statute of Northampton was a general ban on carrying firearms, the example from Massachusetts concerns itself only with people who are armed "offensively"—meaning brandishing a weapon and threateningly pointing it at people, for example. Recall that the Second Amendment was written in part because of the knowledge its creators had about history and the concerns that knowledge gave them about how tyrannical governments wielding significant power might operate. They realized that to be free, people must be able to defend themselves—against one another, sure, but also against agents of the state.

But over time, the "offensive" aspect has been loosened by those who wish to control access to firearms. Instead of weapons being wielded offensively, laws have targeted "offensive weapons"—items that are deemed inherently offensive. And this is no modern invention; clear back in the early 1700s, English legal commentators were making the switch, suggesting that "persons with offensive weapons… may be arrested by the sheriff." Now laws across the country, and the whole world, classify items as "offensive weapons" and limit their use. In many locations, one cannot carry a firearm without the permission of the government, much like King Edward II required nearly a millennia ago.

Gun control has evolved over the years and encompasses a wide range of restrictions: requiring background checks prior to purchase; denying a person the ability to carry a weapon on their person; banning the sale of certain types of guns; requiring firearms to be kept in a safe; imposing a waiting period between purchasing and receiving a firearm; outlawing the private sale of weapons; and limiting the number of rounds a magazine can hold. That last one is especially ludicrous—several states have fixated on this approach to deterring mass shootings, yet these posturing politicians fail to realize that imposing an arbitrary limit on magazine capacity does nothing to improve safety when a person can quickly swap out an empty magazine for another that is full.

Despite the obvious flaws in their position, gun control advocates nevertheless persist, their passions inflamed by the seeming barrage of stories in the media about mass shootings (despite such shootings comprising only a very small percentage of overall homicides). The debate around mass shootings is muddied because different organizations and countries use different definitions of what qualifies. The Gun Violence Archive, for example, considers a mass shooting to be four or more people shot or killed, excluding the shooter. Scrolling through their website, where they compile a list of all such shootings, a trend quickly becomes apparent: most of the shootings are taking place in progressive urban areas in Democratic stronghold states—deep blue, leftist-controlled governments that impose a variety of gun control restrictions. Why would that be? Why would the very places that have the most gun control see the most gun crimes? The paradox here is hard to ignore. If gun control laws were effective, wouldn't these areas see a reduction in gun violence? The reality suggests that simply passing laws doesn't stop those who are intent on breaking them. Criminals, by definition, don't follow laws. When law-abiding citizens are disarmed, they become easy targets for those who disregard the rules; many mass shootings, like in the examples shared previously, take place at schools and other locations that are declared "gun-free zones." All predators prefer places with vulnerable prey.

Another pattern seen in most mass shootings has nothing to do with the guns themselves. Nearly every mass shooting incident in the last three decades—along with many isolated shootings and suicides—all share one thing in common, and it's not the weapons used. Mountains of evidence make clear that these individuals were actively or recently using powerful psychotropic drugs—mind-altering substances that affected their thoughts and actions. And yet the gun control community turns a blind eye to this common denominator, choosing instead to pursue policies that are ineffective in deterring criminals (who, again, don't care to follow laws) while imposing burdens on law-abiding citizens who simply desire to defend themselves against gun-wielding criminals. Restricting access to firearms does not address the root causes of violence.

Why is it the Worst Idea?

When forty-four-year-old Steve Lamar Goss, Jr. decided to break into a home in Mississippi, he tried going through the front door. It was locked, and his best efforts to kick the door down didn't work. The husband was away from work, with his wife and three children in the home. Terrified by the pounding at the door, the woman alerted her husband and hid in a closet with her kids. While the husband called 911 to alert the police, Goss got in his truck and drove it directly into the dining room, busting through the home's outer wall to let himself in. Armed with a knife, he began searching the house. The mom and her children were discovered by the intruder just minutes later; the police had not yet arrived. When Goss opened the closet, still wielding his knife, the mom shot him in the arm, and he fled.

What might have happened had she not been armed? Those situations are too frequent to ponder; disarmed people are unable to defend themselves and fall prey to their predators. History is full of such examples, from single-death encounters to mass murders of disarmed citizens by their own totalitarian governments. In the twentieth century alone, some 262 million people were killed that way, in what's called democide—the intentional killing of an unarmed person or people by their government. And this is why gun control is such an evil—it incapacitates people, allowing criminals (including those in the government) to gain more power over them. It is precisely why the founders crafted the Second Amendment to the US Constitution—not simply to protect people's ability to hunt animals or even to fight back against home intruders, but also to fight back against tyrants and deter their rise in power. It's hard to kill millions of people who can shoot back at the soldiers sent to murder them. As the saying goes, an armed society is a polite society. Widespread gun ownership among the citizenry helps keep the peace.

Someone might push back against these arguments by saying that this is why we have police—highly trained individuals whose job it is to keep the peace and keep us safe. But this is a foolish view of what the police are and do. Consider the example just shared: Goss was not deterred by armed police officers, who hadn't even shown up yet. Average response times when you call 911 vary based on what city you're in and can range from five minutes to over an hour or more. When seconds matter, police are only minutes away. This means they don't exist to protect you—they largely exist to investigate a crime *after* it has occurred. And even when they do show up on time, they are under no obligation to actually help. A well-known example graphically illustrates a common policy across the USA. On March 16, 1975, two men broke into a three-story home in Washington, D.C. A woman on the second floor was assaulted, and her two housemates on the floor above her heard her screams. They called 911, and police were dispatched to check out the incident. After knocking on the door and receiving no answer, the police left the scene. The frantic housemates called 911 a second time. The dispatcher promised the women that help would come, but no officers were even sent. The attackers discovered the housemates, and all three women were assaulted over the next fourteen hours. When they later sued the city and its police department for failing to protect them and not even responding to their second call, the court dismissed the case, stating that the police have no duty to help individuals and only exist to provide services to the "public at large." There exists a "fundamental principle," argued the court, "that a government and its agents are under no general duty to provide public services, such as police protection, to any particular individual citizen." The government "assumes a duty only to the public at large and not to individual members of the community." This is not just the opinion of a few judges but a pervasive policy regarding police services throughout the nation. Police don't have to protect you; we're on our own and should act accordingly.

The consequences of gun control are not just theoretical—they are real and often devastating. From tyrannical governments to everyday criminals, those who wish to inflict harm are emboldened when they know their victims are defenseless. Gun control laws create a false sense of security while failing to address the true sources of violence. They ignore the fundamental right to self-defense and the historical lessons that have repeatedly shown the dangers of disarmament. There are few worse ways for a government to harm its citizens than to impede their ability to protect themselves.

A World Without It

Police officers are a modern invention, created in the mid-1800s as urbanization prompted the creation of centralized, taxpayer-funded law-enforcement agencies. Previously, those who kept the peace were typically informal, privately funded constables and militiamen. In the absence of modern police forces, communities relied heavily on personal responsibility and communal cooperation to maintain order. The right to bear arms wasn't just a constitutional formality—it was a practical necessity and part of maintaining order. Everyone played a role in ensuring the safety and security of their neighborhood, and being armed was a critical component of that responsibility. Every male (at the time) was effectively considered part of the militia, so when the founders wrote, in the Second Amendment, that the right to keep and bear arms shall not be infringed because "a well regulated militia" was necessary to their security, they were referring not to police officers or soldiers or government agents. They were referring to everyone. The right to keep and bear arms is an individual one.

A world without gun control is one where criminals would think twice more often before attempting a break-in or an assault, knowing that there is a good chance their intended victims are likely armed and capable of defending themselves. So-called "gun-free zones" would be a thing of the past, depriving homicidal maniacs of the benefit of a shooting spree at easy targets. These deterrents would significantly reduce crime rates, as the risk associated with criminal activities would be much higher. Law-abiding citizens, equipped with the means to protect themselves, would create a safer and more resilient community.

Abolishing gun control laws would also deter dictators and oppressive governments of all stripes, ensuring that would-be despots are restrained in their ability to control their citizens. The widespread democide of the twentieth century would be a relic of history since armed people would have the opportunity to rise up against their oppressors. More importantly, those oppressors would be disincentivized to initiate force because of the concern about being shot at by an armed individual. When the government deprives its citizens of means of protection and hoards to itself and its agents (soldiers, police, etc.) all the weapons, this creates a power imbalance and creates untold victims. Removing gun control laws helps balance the scale of power and creates a far better equilibrium.

Because we would no longer be performing "security theater"—pretending that gun control laws actually limit violence and deter criminals—more energy and attention could be focused on psychotropic medication and its use, especially by young people. We would focus on preventative measures and the proliferation of personal responsibility instead of satisfying ourselves with purely punitive measures after the fact. By shifting our focus from superficial measures to the underlying causes of violent behavior, we can make meaningful progress in preventing tragedies before they occur. And by promoting personal responsibility and responsible gun ownership, more people would be educated, trained, and, therefore, able to step in and deter a would-be shooter—including teachers at school, arming themselves to defend the children in their care.

In a world without gun control, we would live in a society that recognizes that gun control is not about guns—it's about control. By abolishing these horrendous laws, we reclaim our autonomy and enjoy an increase in freedom. Individuals would be empowered to take responsibility for their own safety, fostering a culture of vigilance and self-reliance. Without the constraints of gun control, we would see a society where personal liberty thrives and communities are strengthened through mutual support and shared responsibility. This shift would dismantle the illusion of state-provided safety and highlight the importance of individual actors standing up to preserve freedom. In short, a world without gun control is a world inhabited by free people.

Tuttle Twins Takeaways

1. The Second Amendment was designed to ensure individuals could defend themselves not just from criminals but from potential government tyranny.

2. Gun control laws do not prevent criminals, who by definition do not follow laws, from obtaining and using firearms.

3. "Gun-free zones" often become targets for mass shootings because they ensure victims are defenseless.

4. Disarming law-abiding citizens makes them easy targets for criminals.

5. Gun control creates a false sense of security and does not address the root causes of violence.

MINIMUM WAGE

When the government makes it illegal
to pay someone a low wage, low-skilled
workers often lose their jobs entirely
instead of being paid more.

" Those who advocate
higher minimum wages
must face the reality that
they are simply pricing the
lowest-skilled workers out
of the job market."

~ Barry Goldwater

On a warm spring afternoon in New York City, March 25, 1911, smoke began billowing from the eighth floor of the Asch Building in Greenwich Village. Inside, nearly 500 workers, mostly young Italian and Jewish immigrant women, were nearing the end of another grueling work-day at the Triangle Shirtwaist Factory. As flames engulfed the building, panic set in. The girls' screams, floors above the street below, could be heard above the noise of approaching fire engines and police patrol wagons. Twenty-four-year-old Yetta Lubitz found herself trapped on the ninth floor. The stairway door was locked—a common practice by factory owners to prevent theft and unauthorized breaks—enabling them to check the women's purses prior to leaving the building. Fire escapes buckled under the weight of fleeing workers. Lubitz and some of the girls worked their way to the roof and saved themselves in the process. Unfortunately, many others did not. The fire caused the deaths of 146 workers—either from the fire itself, smoke inhalation, or jumping to their deaths; most of the victims were teenagers.

This horrifying tragedy brought national attention to the conditions faced by these workers in an industrial age where people were eager for employment, even at low wages. The workers in the Triangle factory, for example, worked nine hours a day plus seven hours on Saturdays, earning a total of around $10 per week for their time and effort—the equivalent of around $6 per hour in today's dollars. Their cause was taken up by Frances Perkins, a worker's rights advocate who was appalled at what she saw and the consequences of what she felt were too few laws and regulations to protect workers. Perkins' political activism took off as she assumed various leadership positions in labor organizations, ultimately getting close to the then-governor of New York, Franklin D. Roosevelt. The governor appointed her as the state's first industrial commissioner, overseeing 1,800 bureaucrats in the new office. When Roosevelt assumed the presidency shortly thereafter, he took Perkins with him, appointing her to his cabinet—making her the first female cabinet member in US history. She presented Roosevelt with a list of labor reforms she would plan to fight for and implement—sweeping changes to employment law in the country. "Nothing like this has ever been done in the United States before," she told him. "You know that, don't you?" He agreed and made her his Secretary of Labor.

Among the reforms Perkins pushed was a minimum wage law—an effort to ensure that workers would be guaranteed a "living wage" sufficient to provide for their needs. The concept of a minimum wage was not entirely new. As early as 1912, Massachusetts had passed a law recommending wages for women and children, though it wasn't mandatory. But Perkins envisioned a federal mandate that would apply across the nation, setting a floor for wages in all industries. And FDR was alongside her effort, soliciting political support for the cause. "Something has to be done about... starvation wages," he said on the campaign trail. The foundation was being laid for a new federal law that would impose a minimum wage requirement across industries in an effort to provide workers with enough income to get along in life. But as with many other government reforms, these good intentions could not stop the negative consequences from coming.

The Context

Senator Hugo Black, a Democrat, had little influence in Congress during his first term in office, when Republicans held control of both chambers. But the 1932 election swung the pendulum in his favor, delivering to Democrats a majority in Congress as well as the presidency, with the election of Black's friend, FDR. Seizing this opportunity, Black drafted a bill to create a minimum wage guarantee for workers—a bill that also aimed to limit the workweek to thirty hours. The bill received significant pushback and did not pass that year, nor in the few years that followed. But with Perkins and her allies helping behind the scenes, six years later, a revised version of that same bill (adopting an eight-hour day and a forty-hour workweek, also establishing the minimum wage) did pass through Congress.

The night before he signed the Fair Labor Standards Act, FDR held a "fireside chat" to speak with the public. Remarking on this bill—which he later called the most important piece of New Deal legislation since the Social Security Act three years prior—he said, "Do not let any calamity-howling executive with an income of $1,000 a day... tell you... that a wage of [25 cents an hour] is going to have a disastrous effect on all American industry." The Great Depression had provided the political environment necessary to pass a law of this type, and Perkins and allies twisted enough arms to make the vote pass. This law changed the entire employment culture of the United States, and countless workers rejoiced at finally securing a guarantee that they would be paid "fair" wages, sufficient to provide for their personal needs.

As the dollar has been debased for decades, Congress has had to repeatedly adjust the minimum wage amount since inflation obviously makes it ridiculous for a person to continue earning 25 cents per hour today. Most recently, the law was changed in 2009 to set the minimum wage at $7.25 per hour. While a significant change at the time, this latest increase, in the wake of a global financial crisis, soon became a focal point of criticism. Activists began pushing for a $15 per hour minimum wage in a "fight for fifteen," arguing that it was necessary to lift millions of workers out of poverty and reduce income inequality. A meager seven bucks just wasn't enough.

These activists' efforts fell on deaf ears federally, so they took their fight to cities and states around the country. And just as the Fair Labor Standards Act only passed with Democrats in control, the activists pushing for increasing the minimum wage today have seen success in targeting jurisdictions with Democrat strongholds: California, New York, Massachusetts, New Jersey, Washington, Maryland, etc. Many of these governments have gone one step further, tying their minimum wage rates to inflation in order to automatically keep pace with the cost of living.

The scales tipped in 2013 when Kshama Sawant, a member of the Socialist Alternative revolutionary movement, was elected to the Seattle city council. She had made the minimum wage—specifically, increasing it to $15 per hour—the cornerstone of her campaign. And in May, hundreds of fast-food workers in the city went on strike—Seattle being one of sixty cities that took part in the coordinated strike—demanding higher pay and bringing attention to their plight. Building off of the momentum that swept her into victory, Sawant and her allies obtained enough votes from the council to pass the first $15 per hour minimum wage law in any major city in the country.

From there, other cities and states have followed suit, responding to rising demand for rising wages, especially in an environment of high inflation. A Pew Research Center poll in 2021 found that 62 percent of American voters say they favor raising the federal minimum wage to $15 an hour, including 40 percent who strongly back the idea. But even this effort soon becomes unsatisfying to some of its chief proponents. Consider Representative Rashida Tlaib of Michigan, a longtime supporter of increasing the minimum wage. "When we started [the fight for an increased minimum wage], it should have been $15," she said. "Now I think… it should be $20 an hour." Why stop there? Why not $22 or $30 or $50 per hour? If increasing the minimum wage has no apparent downsides—at least, none that are admitted to by advocates—then what's to stop us from raising the minimum to much higher amounts? As Walter Williams once wrote, "All these good intentions of the champions of minimum-wage raises do nothing to cure [the] evil consequences…" And boy, are there consequences.

Why is it the Worst Idea?

Once Seattle passed its minimum wage law, one local business owner said that "when we projected out the minimum wage increases… we realized we would be functionally bankrupt if you were to fast forward seven years in the future." California, eager to be boldly progressive compared to its peers, passed a $20 minimum wage for fast-food workers. And in the months that followed, nearly 10,000 jobs were eliminated as a direct result. Pizza Hut laid off 1,200 drivers; Rubio's closed forty-eight locations, firing all their staff due to the "rising cost of doing business"; and El Pollo Loco and Jack in the Box announced that they will speed up the use of robotics, including robots that make salsa and cook fried foods. Across the state, fast-food companies passed on the increased personnel costs to customers by raising prices. Less than a month later, Wendy's had increased prices by 8 percent, Chipotle's prices increased by 7.5 percent, and Starbucks prices increased by 7 percent. McDonald's has announced it will be raising prices, and many other fast-food franchises have announced hiring freezes. But price increases can only go so far, as upset customers might look elsewhere or cook more meals at home. "I can't charge $20 for Happy Meals," noted one McDonald's franchisee in California. And when costs are high (due to minimum wage laws, among other factors) and those costs can't be passed on to willing customers, businesses shrink or shut down.

These are just a few of the consequences of making major, arbitrary economic changes. After California's new law, the Arby's in Hollywood on Sunset Boulevard closed after fifty-five years of operation. "With minimum wage going up, and the customer count going down, it's a really tough business to be in right now," the general manager told a reporter. Out of the twenty employees working at the restaurant, ten of them had worked there for over a decade. Now, they were all out of a job. This consequence is consistent with what many economists warned about and have since studied. One review of the data from Seattle's minimum wage hike identified a "decline in hours [worked] that is of larger magnitude than the estimated positive effect on wages, suggesting that the amount paid to low-wage workers fell." In other words, while some people remained employed and were paid more as a result of the law, other workers had their hours cut or lost their jobs—and the net effect of the law was negative, despite it being positive for some. Another group of economists reviewed a variety of studies on minimum wage laws and their effects and concluded that "the evidence still shows that minimum wages pose a tradeoff of higher wages for some against job losses for others." Some win, and many others lose. It's not the utopia that advocates always claim it is.

This is why minimum wage laws are so atrocious—they hold appeal for those who can still hold down a job, but they ignore the reality that increasing the amount prices some people out of work. It's a political manipulation of economic exchange, distorting the market and wreaking fiscal havoc on many businesses. Sure, many people don't like to think that anyone's labor might be worth less than the minimum wage, but it's true. Consider someone flipping burgers; one might think this person deserves a "living wage" and should be paid $15 per hour or more. But if that worker's actions only create $7 worth of value per hour to the business, the owner cannot justify employing them and paying them more than the value they bring. So businesses fire humans and introduce automation that is cheaper—leading the intended beneficiaries of the law high and dry, out of work altogether. Minimum wage laws are a solution that simply creates more problems.

People respond to incentives. When business owners are compelled to pay people more than they're worth—rather, more than the value they bring to the business—then they are incentivized to find alternative options to drive costs down in order to remain profitable. This is why restaurants are switching to automation so heavily. And this ultimately means that low-skilled, inexperienced individuals—such as teenagers—are deprived of opportunities to enter the market and build experience. Minimum wage laws are like taking a big ladder, sawing off the bottom two rungs, gluing them to the top, and then patting yourself on the back for increasing the height of the ladder. In reality, you've removed the ability for people to take their first steps upward. And the higher the minimum wage, the higher the incentive for businesses to accelerate automation and eliminate low-skilled positions. It's one thing to celebrate the recent college graduate working a barista job who will get a few more dollars per hour now—that's the consequence that is visible and celebrated. It's another thing to understand that reality requires us to see the *unseen* consequences—the ones that advocates don't want you to pay attention to. In this case, it's people like the high school senior looking to get a job and save up for their future—these people are negatively impacted, yet their plight is ignored by those who remain fixated on increasing the minimum wage.

Here's a simple and blunt truth: the real minimum wage is zero. That is the amount many low-skilled and inexperienced people receive as a result of legislation that makes it illegal to pay them what they are currently worth to a business. Thomas Sowell, the famed economist, once wrote that "no one is employable or unemployable absolutely, but only relative to a given pay scale." People are employable if they create value, and they are going to be compensated at an amount that can be justified. Someone with no skills is largely unemployable, except for low-paying positions where they can gain experience and develop skills to become more employable. Even *The New York Times* once agreed with this simple premise. In a 1987 editorial, the paper wrote, "There's a virtual consensus among economists that the minimum wage is an idea whose time has passed. Raising the minimum wage by a substantial amount would price working poor people out of the job market."

Minimum wage laws, despite their superficial appeal, are a cruel deception that hurts the very people they claim to help. They are a blunt instrument wielded by politicians who ignore economic realities and the devastating consequences of their actions. These laws don't just eliminate jobs; they eliminate hope and opportunity for countless individuals seeking to climb the economic ladder. By artificially inflating wages, we don't create prosperity—we create unemployment, automation, and economic stagnation. We rob young people of crucial early work experiences, deprive low-skilled workers of a chance to prove their worth, and force small businesses to shutter their doors. The minimum wage is a feel-good policy that allows politicians to pat themselves on the back while leaving a trail of economic destruction in their wake.

A World Without It

Teenagers aren't the only ones competing for low-skilled jobs at the bottom rung of the economic ladder—so are convicted felons. After a stint in prison for filing fraudulent tax returns and netting over a million dollars in undeserved refunds, Claudia Shivers took a job at the local coffee shop, working for $9.34 per hour. This was a drastic career shift from her past life as an accountant and one that she struggled to maintain. "It was a struggle because I was no longer able to work in the financial sector," Shivers wrote. "No one trusted me." So she served coffee for hardly enough money to get by. "I had a rocky start and there were several times I thought I might get fired because I had no idea what a latte was, much less how to steam milk." She lacked experience and, therefore, did not create much value for her employer. She was paid what she was worth at the time.

But that bottom rung of the ladder allowed Shivers to get a foothold and push herself back up, moving beyond her criminal past. Using the knowledge and experience she had gained in an entirely new line of work, she launched her own business, Queen Coffee Bean. "When I wake up every day, I have another opportunity to live my dream," she wrote. "I serve coffee to people who empathize with my past and support my business, but wouldn't hire me to work at theirs." It was a low-paying job that enabled her to enter the market and rebuild her life. That is the vision of a world without minimum wage laws—it's a world where the bottom runs of the economic ladder are firmly in place, welcoming everyone seeking to gain experience, develop skills, and make themselves more marketable by creating value for their employers.

Boosting the skills and productivity of workers is the only viable way to boost their wages. By setting aside political "solutions" such as minimum wage laws, we would be able to focus our energy and attention on actual solutions to help low-skilled people improve their economic opportunities, such as:

- Encouraging businesses to create apprenticeship programs that combine on-the-job training with classroom instruction so people can earn while they learn, gaining valuable skills and experience without the burden of student debt.

- Offering microloans for people looking to launch their own small business like Shivers, paired with mentorship programs to empower them to create their own economic opportunities.

- The gig economy, where individuals can offer their services—such as driving people or delivering food—on their own time and terms, enabling them to develop several streams of revenue without having to be someone else's employee.

- Raising awareness of job opportunities that use a skills-based hiring practice instead of requiring a college degree, to open doors for talented individuals who may lack formal credentials.

- Promoting a "try before you hire" program for businesses to offer short-term, project-based opportunities for unskilled workers to prove their potential and gain experience, with the possibility of full-time employment for those who excel.

It would be great to compensate everyone at a high rate, but to do so, they must create enough value to merit that level of pay; simply paying all workers more would cause more businesses to fail. Good intentions don't suspend basic economic realities. Just as you can't legislate that a farmer grow enough crops to feed his family, you can't legislate that workers earn a "living wage." But what we *can* do is create a working environment that is open to all, regardless of their skill level, so that people can gain experience, build a network, and improve their earning level over time. It requires more patience than simply passing a law to create immediate effect—but it's the right way to do it and the only real way to do it.

In an economy without minimum wage laws, entry-level jobs would once again serve as crucial stepping stones. Young people would find it easier to gain valuable work experience, developing skills and a work ethic that serve them throughout their careers. Businesses, freed from arbitrary wage floors, could invest more in training and expansion, creating more jobs and opportunities for advancement. The labor market would become more dynamic and responsive, with wages reflecting true value and productivity rather than government mandates. Economic struggle and poverty would obviously still exist, but the economy would clearly reward ingenuity, hard work, and personal growth. Instead of relying on well-intentioned but ultimately harmful legislation, we would foster an environment where market-based solutions and individual empowerment drive economic progress. Instead of hurting some people while helping others, we would rather try to help everyone. That's a better world worth fighting for.

Tuttle Twins Takeaways

1. Proponents of minimum wage laws argue they help lift workers out of poverty and reduce income inequality.

2. In reality, these laws lead to job losses, reduced hours, and accelerated automation in low-wage industries.

3. The implementation of minimum wage laws often results in a trade-off: higher wages for some workers at the cost of job losses or reduced opportunities for others.

4. The real minimum wage is effectively zero when workers lose their jobs or can't find employment due to artificially inflated wage floors.

5. Entry-level, low-wage jobs serve as crucial steps on a ladder of economic progress to gain experience and skills, and by enacting arbitrary wage minimums, the bottom rungs of the ladder are cruelly removed.

Your planet is abundant with the most precious element in the universe—the foundation of life, carbon.
Oh, we're actually trying to get rid of it.
...and also enslave mankind.

CLIMATE "CHANGE"

Politicians wanting to tax and control their citizens use the ever-changing weather to scare them into submission and increase support for global government.

> " The environmental movement has been hijacked by political and social activists who are using green rhetoric to advance agendas that have more to do with anti-capitalism than with science or ecology."
>
> ~ Patrick Moore

Lonnie Thompson is a true-life iceman—a famed glaci-ologist who travels the world studying ice. Funded with a $7,000 grant from the National Science Foundation in 1974, Thompson led a scouting party to Quelccaya, an ancient volcanic plain 18,000 feet above sea level. Their mission: to remove an ice core and study its contents for signs of historical climate change. Thompson's efforts were a success, leading him to be the first scientist to retrieve ice samples from a remote tropical ice cap. In the decades since, he has led scores of expeditions to ice fields in sixteen countries on a quest, as his biographer put it, "to solve the riddle of climate change." Thompson's consistent conclusion was that Earth's ice record showed huge swings in the climate—dry spells followed by wet spells with large lakes coming and going in the valleys. Dust from the dried lakebeds left their signal in the ice. The ice samples—"ca-naries in the coalmine," as Thompson put it—were clear indicators of a climate catastrophe. Speaking to a group of peer climatologists, Thompson remarked that "Virtually all of us are now convinced that global warming poses a clear and present danger to civilization." But few outside of these scientific fields were listening.

That would change many years after Thompson's work soon began, with the release of *An Inconvenient Truth*, a film produced by former U.S. Vice President Al Gore in 2006. This documentary brought widespread public atten-tion to the issue of global warming and climate change. The film presented Gore's slideshow on climate change, which he had been delivering for years, to a much broad-er audience. It combined statistical models, photographs of melting glaciers, personal anecdotes, and predictions about the future impacts of climate change. The film's release marked a turning point in public awareness of climate change. It grossed nearly $50 million worldwide—making it the eleventh highest-grossing documentary in the United States—and won two Academy Awards, sparking intense debate and discussion about climate change in mainstream media, politics, and public discourse.

Thompson wasn't able to attend the premiere, as he was on a journey to South America to retrieve another ice sample. But he was content with the film, which heavily featured his work, because he felt it did what he and his peers had been unable to do themselves: "It got climate change on the radar," he said. Summarizing the findings of hundreds of researchers in his presentation, Gore was adamant that unless we took "drastic measures" to reduce carbon dioxide emissions, the world would reach a "point of no return" in a decade—it was, he said, a "true planetary emergency." For his efforts, he was awarded the Nobel Peace Prize the following year, for his "efforts to build up and disseminate greater knowledge about man-made climate change, and to lay the foundations for the measures that are needed to counteract such change." One climatologist remarked that Gore's film "has had a much greater impact on public opinion and public awareness of global climate change than any scientific paper or report."

That impact was evident through polling and politics. A survey by the Pew Research Center found that in the months following the documentary's release, the percentage of Americans who believed that human activity was responsible for global warming rose from 41 percent to 50 percent. A Stanford University study showed that global warming topped Americans' worries as the largest environmental threat; the number of Americans identifying it as the world's single biggest environmental problem doubled from the prior year. "Climate change now places far ahead of any other environmental problem in the public's mind," the study observed. "Additionally, over 50 percent found the issue personally important, compared to less than 30 percent in 1997." And that was Gore's point—to induce viewers to feel personally connected to and responsible for the crisis, thus (hopefully) prompting action. This groundswell of public attention and interest spilled over into political action. Committees were formed, laws were passed, studies were funded, debates were had, taxes were raised, and thousands of environmentalist bureaucrats were hired by governments across the world to address this "inconvenient truth." For Thompson and his peers, it was a milestone building on their decades of research—finally, those in power were listening! Action would be taken! Somebody would do something about it! Yet Gore himself said that "Ultimately, this is not really a political issue so much as a moral issue. If we allow [global temperatures to increase], it is deeply unethical."

Except, climate change is a *deeply* political issue.

The Context

On a bleak December day in 1620, a small ship called the *Mayflower* anchored near the shore of a vast, untamed land. The passengers, exhausted and hopeful, gazed upon the unfamiliar coastline with a mix of trepidation and anticipation. Among them were the Pilgrims, a group of determined souls seeking freedom from the religious persecution that had hounded them across an ocean. They had endured a grueling journey, braving tempestuous seas and near starvation, driven by an unyielding desire for a new beginning. As they set foot on the cold, rocky ground of what would become Plymouth Rock, they couldn't have known the significance of this moment. This modest landing marked the start of a bold experiment in self-governance and community.

You can see the rock for yourself at Pilgrim Memorial State Park in Plymouth, Massachusetts. It sits on the shore of Plymouth Harbor, at sea level. A granite portico now surrounds it to help preserve it from the elements. Curiously, some observers have noticed the rock remains at sea level, over four centuries later. This is not quite true; the waterfront was renovated in 1920, and the rock was repositioned in the new portico for protection. We can't say, accurately, that the rock is where it was clear back in 1620. Yet a century has passed with it in its current home, and it is not submerged under rising sea levels.

This presents a problem for the climate change comrades. For example, in *An Inconvenient Truth*, Gore warned that due to global warming, melting ice would cause sea levels to rise by 20 feet "in the near future." However, Plymouth Rock's current location and condition suggest that these apocalyptic predictions have not come to pass. It also suggests we should more closely examine the prevailing narratives about climate change, including the claim that the "debate is settled," as President Obama said in 2014. "Climate change is a fact." We can start by looking at who is funding this so-called science.

There are eighteen programs in the federal government dedicated to "addressing climate change." Over $14 billion in taxpayer dollars are spent each year on climate change-related programs, with $154 billion being spent since 1993. But that's nothing compared to what the future holds in store. In June 2024, the White House announced an "Investing in America" agenda, through which "more than $50 billion is being delivered to advance climate adaptation and resilience across the nation." A suite of bills passed by a Democrat-controlled Congress has committed the government to spend more than half a trillion dollars on "climate technology and clean energy" over the next decade. When the Environmental Protection Agency announced $4.3 billion in grant funding being awarded to twenty-five new projects, all of them were to "tackle climate change." In other words, if you want to be a scientist in this field, the gravy train is heading in only one direction; it pays to study what the government supports. As one researcher wrote, "The political realm in turn fed money back into the scientific community. By the late 1990s, lots of jobs depended on the idea that carbon emissions caused global warming." He continued:

> I was on that gravy train, making a high wage in a science job that would not have existed if we didn't believe carbon emissions caused global warming. And so were lots of people around me; there were international conferences full of such people. We had political support, the ear of government, big budgets. We felt fairly important and useful (I did anyway). It was great. We were working to save the planet!

But why would politicians be interested in and supportive of climate change? One simple reason: power. As the authors note in *Hot Talk, Cold Science: Global Warming's Unfinished Debate*, the political class wasn't simply acting upon sound science. Rather, "politics quickly overtook science as environmental advocates and other interest groups recognized the utility of the climate change issue in advancing their own agendas." Most recently, advocates have rallied behind a "Green New Deal," echoing President Franklin D. Roosevelt's totalitarian New Deal a century ago, which manipulated the economy in a variety of ways at the expense of individual freedom. So, too, with the Green version—one espoused by the likes of Representative Alexandria Ocasio-Cortez who said, "This is going to be the New Deal, the Great Society, the moon shot, the civil-rights movement of our generation." But while she gets much of the credit for this proposal—which aims to eliminate the use of fossil fuels in favor of vast networks of solar panels and wind turbines, creating a massive government bureaucracy to manage the entire economy's transition—it was her chief of staff, Saikat Chakrabarti, who was its author. "The interesting thing about the Green New Deal is it wasn't originally a climate thing at all," he once admitted. "Do you guys think of it as a climate thing? Because we really think of it as a how-do-you-change-the-entire-economy thing."

The effort to "tackle climate change" is a money laundering scheme, much like the Military Industrial Complex which financially benefits—and significantly so—from foreign conflict. Advocates love climate hysteria because it increases the justification for funneling billions of dollars to like-minded researchers, advocacy organizations, and institutions. Politicians love it because they can look like they're "saving the Earth" and being productive doing beneficial things—all while enriching their politically connected friends at the expense of their constituents. And remember what governments across the country did in the name of fighting COVID-19 using emergency powers? That's what the most ardent climate change advocates want—the declaration of a "climate emergency" that would essentially give the government a blank check and unlimited power to impose these programs on the public. It is, on the whole, a pursuit of total government control over the nation's economy—dictating what type of food people can eat (since cattle generate "too much" carbon dioxide), whether you can grow a backyard garden (since one study found that homegrown foods produce five times more carbon emissions than industrial farming methods), or how much you can travel (so as to reduce your "carbon footprint"). It is a new religion for those who worship central planning—one where heretics are unwelcome and unable to ask questions. It is anti-freedom.

Why is it the Worst Idea?

If you ask a young person about the Earth's prospects, chances are they won't paint a pretty picture. A recent survey, for example, found that 83 percent of Gen Z Americans—people between the ages of fourteen and twenty-four—are concerned about the health of the planet. 75 percent say their mental health has been affected by the environment. And nearly 60 percent of them say they are "very worried" or "extremely worried" about climate change. There's even a new term for this environmentally induced terror: climate anxiety. It shows up in the attitudes and actions of young people and in the opinions they express when asked for public opinion polls. Three-quarters of this age bracket say they thought the future was frightening. And over half (56 percent) say they think humanity is doomed.

This is the result of fear-based propaganda—the doom-and-gloomers preaching their religion about an approaching environmental apocalypse. It is a crippling, depression-inducing worldview—one that sees humanity as a parasite on an otherwise perfect Earth. Over 40 percent of this demographic say they are hesitant to have children. Thirty-three percent cited climate change as a reason they had, or expected to have, fewer children than they considered ideal. And it's not just the younger adults who have bought into this belief system. Lori Day, a fifty-six-year-old parent, joined a group called BirthStrike, whose members pledge to abstain from having children because of "the severity of the ecological crisis." She shared with the group that though she used to yearn to be a grandmother, her daughter had decided not to have children—a decision that instead brought Day relief. "I would be worried sick," Day said. "It would haunt me." Here is one more of countless such stories that could be shared:

> Mason Cummings, 34, said he almost breaks out in tears when he thinks about his nieces, a 6-year-old and a 3-year-old. Cummings, a producer for the Wilderness Society who lives in Durango, Colo., had a vasectomy in 2016 after deciding that he couldn't "morally bring a child into a world that doesn't have a secure future," he said.

This cause—this religious cult—has been fueled by grassroots groups, well-funded activist organizations, and a complicit media. The "Environment Editor" for *The Guardian*, for example, wrote a post titled "Want to fight climate change? Have fewer children." He cited data that having one fewer child will save 58.6 tons of carbon dioxide each year—dwarfing other actions like recycling, living car-free, switching to an electric vehicle, eating a plant-based diet, or upgrading your light bulbs to LED ones. No wonder so many people have "climate anxiety"—the message has been that humans are a stain on the Earth and that perpetuating our species comes at the expense of our planet's very survival.

But this notion is absolutely, categorically, incorrect. Carbon dioxide is not a pollutant. It is plant food; photosynthesis cannot occur without it. We breathe in oxygen and exhale carbon dioxide. Plants absorb carbon dioxide and give us oxygen. Reducing this essential compound means decreasing food and other organic matter on Earth. Most organisms would disappear. By contrast, additional CO_2 leads to faster-growing plants, which leads to less erosion of topsoil, bigger crop yields, and less water loss. Increased foliage supports diverse ecosystems by providing more habitats and food sources for insects, birds, and other wildlife. Insects, which are critical for pollination and a food source for other animals, thrive in environments with abundant vegetation. Birds benefit from the increased availability of insects and seeds, while animals find more shelter and food. CO_2 is, therefore, the foundation of a virtuous cycle of improvement to an ecosystem—not destruction.

Gore presented *An Inconvenient Truth*; here's an *actual* inconvenient truth. The climate has *always* changed. Before this became the term of choice, the hysteria was focused on "global warming" and singling out CO2 as the cause. As a 2001 *Time* article declared, "Scientists no longer doubt that global warming is happening, and almost nobody questions the fact that humans are at least partly responsible." And yet, just decades prior to that, the hysteria was focused on the opposite: "global cooling." Since 1979, NASA weather data points to a slight warming trend, but as *The New York Times* revealed in 1978, the years just prior produced a different concern: "International Team of Specialists Finds No End in Sight to 30-Year Cooling Trend in Northern Hemisphere," read the headline. Three years earlier, the paper published a review of a book by a climatologist whose warnings about global cooling reflected, the paper wrote, "the consensus of the climatological community." And a year before that, the paper produced an article titled "Scientists Ponder Why World's Climate is Changing; A Major Cooling Widely Considered to Be Inevitable."

But again, this isn't really about the climate—it's about leveraging this Earth-wide concern to advance a political agenda. Here's the former Canadian Minister of the Environment, Christine Stewart, admitting to it: "No matter if the science [of global warming] is all phony... climate change [provides] the greatest chance to bring about justice and equality in the world." Or take former senator Timothy Wirth, who took a job at the United Nations Foundation, where he lobbies for hundreds of billions of US taxpayer dollars to be transferred to poorer countries to "tackle climate change." Or, finally, take Paul Watson, the founder of Greenpeace, a global organization of environmental activists. He said, "It doesn't matter what is true, it only matters what people believe is true." The ends ("saving the planet!") justify the means (lies, deception, power, and control).

This dynamic presents one more way in which climate change is a ridiculous notion—a scam foisted on the duped citizenry. The people who most loudly shame the public for their contributions to "man-made climate change"—including driving in a car, flying in a plane, or eating beef—are profound hypocrites, indulging themselves beyond comparison in these very same areas. Private jets, yachts, lavish meals, and more mean that the elite has the biggest "carbon footprint" yet castigate the rest of us for our comparatively tiny ones. They fly around the world speaking to audiences about the need for sacrifice—eating bugs instead of beef or limiting travel—when they ignore their own counsel. It's austerity for thee but not for me.

The concept of "climate change" is disastrous and misleading. It has been weaponized to instill fear and anxiety, especially among the young, who now believe humanity's very existence and the perpetuation of our species are a threat to the planet. This fear-mongering leads to drastic, misguided policies that prioritize government control and elite agendas over individual freedom and human flourishing. Those promoting "tackling climate change" are tyrants in the making.

A World Without It

A cornerstone goal of climate change activists is "net zero"—decarbonizing the economy enough to offset what amount of carbon dioxide emissions still exist. As the globalist World Economic Forum says, "The\ world needs to find global solutions, by committing to support developing countries' efforts to mitigate and adapt to climate change." This, (unsurprisingly), is nonsense. When you look at the data—and set aside the politically motivated agendas— what you find is that wealthy nations all use high amounts of energy. So-called "developing" countries—those with much higher rates of poverty—all fall at the bottom of the list. They all use less energy—in particular, carbon-laden fossil fuels. Put simply, there is no such thing as a low-energy, rich country. And to achieve "net zero," groups like the World Economic Forum would have the vast majority of the world's poorest countries maintain their poverty.

Imagine snapping your fingers in Thanos-like fashion and making the entire climate change movement disappear. What would be the result? In the short term, we'd have fewer taxes, a smaller government, less propaganda, and a research community that has to pursue science instead of putting out government-approved pseudo-science. But in the long term, we'd have the greatest opportunity that has existed for developing nations to climb the economic ladder and join their wealthier peers. This would be possible because the narrative in governments and media outlets across the world would no longer be suppressing their access to developing energy. No longer would they be restricted and shamed for attempting to do what all other nations have done before them. There would be a pathway to prosperity for the poor—one that relies on carbon and its dense energy, far greater than any "renewable" energy resource like solar or wind.

Another consequence of abolishing this atrocious agenda is dismantling the doom-and-gloom outlook on humanity itself. "Climate anxiety" would be a ridiculous thing of the past—an epoch of history we would soon rather forget for its absurdity. Young people, free from the incessant fear-mongering, would instead be empowered with hope and ambition. They would focus on innovation, entrepreneurship, and personal growth rather than living in fear of an impending environmental apocalypse. Social and cultural dynamics would shift toward optimism and human achievement. The narrative of humanity being a destructive force would be replaced with one of potential and creativity. People would recognize that human ingenuity is the key to overcoming challenges, not the cause of them. And free from their apocalyptic anxiety, young people would have more children. This means growing society instead of shrinking it and giving birth to more humans, among whom might be future innovators who bring the world even more wisdom and wealth.

A world liberated from the shackles of climate change hysteria is one where we would enjoy an unprecedented renaissance of human potential and progress. The arbitrary limits on energy use and economic growth would vanish, allowing the poorest among us to rise and achieve their full potential. This is the world we should strive for—one where the promise of human flourishing is fulfilled, unencumbered by the myths of climate catastrophe and the tyrannical mandates to which they inevitably lead.

Tuttle Twins Takeaways

1. Climate change activism promotes fear and anxiety, especially among young people, leading to a pessimistic worldview.

2. The climate change movement is heavily funded and driven by political agendas rather than unbiased scientific inquiry.

3. Climate change policies lead to increased government control and reduced individual freedom, making them a favorite tool of tyrants.

4. The narrative of imminent climate catastrophe has been historically inconsistent, with past predictions of global cooling and warming failing to materialize.

5. Individual freedom and market-driven solutions are more effective in addressing environmental concerns than top-down governmental mandates.

IMMUNITY

Allowing government officials to escape accountability for their harmful actions creates a perverse incentive that may actually increase harmful behavior.

"We are fast approaching the stage of the ultimate inversion: The stage where the government is free to do anything it pleases, while the citizens may act only by permission."

~ Ayn Rand

Baby "Beau," like hundreds of millions of babies before and since, received a suite of vaccinations as an infant. Born in 1974, Beau was given, among others, the DPT vaccine—created to prevent diphtheria, tetanus, and pertussis, commonly called whooping cough. Shortly afterward, Beau's parents reported that he had "screaming fits" for two days and ran a 103-degree fever, making "jerking movements while sleeping." When he was about four months old, doctors continued the vaccination regimen, administering another DPT shot. Beau started suffering seizures shortly thereafter. He became brain damaged and was still in diapers, able to only say a single word, as an eleven-year-old when his parents sued and were awarded $3.5 million in damages. Theirs became the third DPT malpractice lawsuit to be tried in the country, with many more settled out of court.

Between 1980 and 1986, people claiming their children were injured or killed due to a vaccine brought over three billion dollars of damages claims to civil courts across the country, hoping to hold vaccine manufacturers accountable. This torrent of lawsuits made it difficult for manufacturers to obtain cost-effective liability insurance, leading the companies to either stop production or raise their prices substantially. For example, Wyeth Laboratories stopped producing their DPT vaccine in 1984 "because of extreme liability exposure, cost of litigation, and the difficulty of continuing to obtain adequate insurance." By 1985, only four manufacturers produced the primary vaccines required by states, which had all created laws making vaccination a prerequisite for attending government schools, with limited exceptions afforded. The reduction of available vaccines led public health officials to worry, pressuring Congress to take action.

In 1986, Congress passed—and President Ronald Reagan signed into law—the National Childhood Vaccine Injury Act (NCVIA), which gave vaccine manufacturers almost total immunity for their vaccines, meaning that individuals would no longer be allowed to sue them in civil court unless they could prove that the vaccine was inherently dangerous and that the manufacturer was negligent. This blanket protection largely removed the need for liability insurance or legal fees, thus incentivizing them to continue to produce vaccinations. The statute reads, in part:

> No vaccine manufacturer shall be liable in a civil action for damages arising from a vaccine-related injury or death associated with the administration of a vaccine after October 1, 1988, if the injury or death resulted from side effects that were unavoidable even though the vaccine was properly prepared and was accompanied by proper directions and warnings.

Attorneys with the Justice Department wanted the bill to stop there, closing the doors of civil court to parents of injured children without the opportunity for recourse or damages. Over their objections, a group of parents of vaccine-injured children successfully fought for the creation of a no-fault compensation system as an alternative. Thus, the National Vaccine Injury Compensation Program was created, allowing families to file a claim within three years of the vaccine's administration to their child if they have reason to believe that their child has been injured as a result. The claims that are funded are paid for through an excise tax on vaccines—75 cents added to the cost of each vaccine administered. That means, of course, that the families whose children are injured by a vaccine are compensated not by the manufacturers but by all other families who are required to pay the increased fee to fund the compensation program.

Congress went one step further in 2005, augmenting the liability protections in the NCVIA. Whereas the prior law primarily focused on childhood vaccines, the Public Readiness and Emergency Preparedness Act (PREP) covers a wider range of vaccines used during declared public health emergencies, expanding the scope of which manufacturers are given this legal protection. The stated intent of the bill was to combat unexpected emergencies, accelerating the production of new medical countermeasures, whether a vaccine or other medication or device. But the bill allows common diseases to be used as a reason to provide these companies immunity.

When COVID-19 spread across the globe, the PREP law was used to extend immunity coverage to manufacturers to accelerate the production of an untested vaccine. The Health and Human Services Secretary, as outlined in the law, invoked its power to extend this protection beginning in 2020, lasting for four years. That means that companies like Pfizer and Moderna cannot be sued in court. The same model has been extended elsewhere, for example, with Purdue Pharma—the massive manufacturer behind OxyContin—being given immunity in exchange for paying several billion dollars to state governments to help "fight the opioid epidemic." That means while government budgets grow larger, private parties (*i.e.*, family members of victims) are denied recourse to receive damages.

Okay, so private pharmaceutical companies can't be held accountable by the victims of their products. Surely, though, in a system that requires the "consent of the governed," as the Declaration of Independence states, and one where the First Amendment to the US Constitution protects the right "to petition the government for a redress of grievances"—surely, in such a system, victims would be able to sue the Food and Drug Administration, right? After all, this is the agency responsible for overseeing the efficacy and approving the use of vaccines and medicines. If they are the primary guardians of public health, one would be able to challenge their actions to seek redress, right? Wrong. Because of a legal doctrine called "sovereign immunity," the FDA is protected from personal injury lawsuits.

The Context

"The king can do no wrong." So goes the argument behind sovereign immunity—the idea that the government can do no wrong and cannot be sued by those who have been harmed by its actions. This legal concept dates back to the early monarchy in England, where kings could not be sued in their own courts. Think of it: these kings did some pretty horrible things, and if their subjects could hold them accountable in court, as one historian said, the monarchs "would have passed [their lives] as defendant," continually fighting off lawsuits. From this immunity developed the idea of *rex non potest peccare*, meaning "the king can do no wrong." Initially, this concept referred directly to the individual serving as king, not to the government over which he ruled. Here's how the famous English judge William Blackstone explained it:

> Besides the attribute of sovereignty, the law also ascribes to the king in his political capacity absolute

> perfection. The king can do no wrong.... The king,
> moreover, is not only incapable of doing wrong, but
> even of thinking wrong: he can never mean to do an
> improper thing: in him is no folly or weakness.

Eventually, the idea of *personal* immunity held by the king
was merged into *political* immunity for the government as
a whole. It wasn't just that the king could do no wrong, but
that the government in general held the same status. This
idea, born in England, spread to the American colonists—
former British subjects themselves. Sovereign immunity
persisted through the creation of the Constitution. Alexander Hamilton wrote that "It is inherent in the nature
of sovereignty, not to be amenable [subject] to the [law]
suit of an individual without its consent." James Madison
agreed: "It is not in the power of individuals to call any
state into court." And John Marshall, the first chief justice
of the U.S. Supreme Court, echoed this sentiment: "It is
not rational to suppose that the sovereign power should be
dragged before a court."

In the United States, as in many countries, there is no
monarch; no "king [who] can do no wrong." As a result,
the concept of immunity rests with the governmental entity itself. But what about those who work for the
government—individual actors who may cause harm to
others? Consider one example: On the night of March 23,
2010, Israel Leija was fleeing the police in Tulsa, Texas. As
he careened down the freeway, Chadrin Mullenix, a law
enforcement officer, was positioned on an overpass, his
rifle aimed below. Despite a spike strip being placed ahead
of Leija on the road, which would have surely led to his
car quickly stopping to function, Mullenix—without any

order to do so or any training for this situation—opened fire on the passing vehicle and shot Leija four times, killing him. Leila's family sued Mullenix, arguing that excessive force was used, and the case ended up in the United States Supreme Court with the question of whether the officer was entitled to immunity for his actions. In an 8–1 ruling, the Court decided in favor of Mullenix, arguing that he benefited from *qualified* immunity.

Qualified immunity only came onto the scene three decades prior. In a landmark 1982 Supreme Court case, *Harlow v. Fitzgerald*, the Court decided that government employees should enjoy similar immunity protections as government entities do. Now the historical benefits of the king extended down to the many employees of government, even if they cause harm to others. When Amy Corbitt's ten-year-old son was shot in the back of his knee by a police officer who was instead trying to shoot the family's nearby dog that was approaching him, the courts ruled the same way—as they consistently have in recent decades—that the family would receive no compensation for the injury, despite arguing the officer had used excessive force. The doors to the court were closed since the person who had caused them harm was an employee of the government. As *Reuters* concluded, qualified immunity "has become a nearly failsafe tool to let police brutality go unpunished and deny victims their constitutional rights."

It gets worse: the courts do allow government agents to be sued and held accountable—creating a tiny hole in the wall shielding the government, through which plaintiffs can attempt to navigate. But in order to succeed, they must show that the government employee violated a "clearly established" law that a previous court ruling had recognized. In Leila's case, that meant there needed to be a law specifically prohibiting officers from shooting at cars from freeway overpasses. (There wasn't.) In Corbitt's case, that meant there needed to be a "clearly established" law saying that someone has the right to not be accidentally shot by police. (There wasn't.) In a system meant to uphold justice, immunity has instead become a shield to defend injustice, protecting those in power at the expense of the people they are meant to serve.

Why is it the Worst Idea?

The government is not *entirely* cruel. Plaintiffs who can demonstrate a violation of clearly established law can still have their day in court, though they face an uphill battle using the government (courts) to hold the government (employees) accountable. Or when pharmaceutical companies were shielded from liability, the National Vaccine Injury Compensation Program was an olive branch to harmed families, promising compensation for those whose children were harmed by vaccines. Sure, this program has paid out over $4 billion since it began in 1988. On paper, this looks like some amount of justice is being served—even if other vaccine customers are forced to foot the bill. But the reality is far darker: over 94 percent of families filing a claim with this program are denied. Fewer than six percent receive any form of compensation. There's no right to a fair hearing or actually receiving compensation to care for your injured child. In the words of one attorney specializing in this field of law, "You have the right to fail [a claim]. And you have the right to lose."

Immunity distorts incentives. If I know I might be held legally and financially accountable for my conduct, I am incentivized to only offer helpful products and services—to do no harm to others as I interact with them in society. But if I know that I can do bad things, even accidentally, and get away with it, I am incentivized to let my guard down a bit—to be a bit less cautious in my approach. Or, if I'm a malicious person, I am incentivized to proceed with my dastardly deeds, on the bet that I'll get away with it. A legal system offering immunity like this is fundamentally flawed because it undermines personal responsibility and accountability—core principles of a free society. When government entities or their employees are shielded from consequences, they are less incentivized to act responsibly and ethically. This lack of accountability breeds a culture of impunity, where public officials can engage in misconduct without fear of repercussions, knowing that the law will protect them.

The existence of such protections also perpetuates a two-tiered system of justice, where government officials and private entities with special protections are not held to the same standards as ordinary citizens. This creates an unjust hierarchy, where some are above the law while others are held to stringent standards. It sends a dangerous message that some people's rights and safety are less important than others', depending on who is responsible for the harm. Immunity also undermines the foundational principle of equality before the law. In a just society, everyone—regardless of their position or status—should be held accountable for their actions. But immunity creates a legal shield for certain individuals and entities, allowing them to evade responsibility. This selective protection not only erodes public trust but also rightly fosters resentment and cynicism among citizens who see a system rigged in favor of the powerful. Imagine being the family member of a victim wrongly harmed or killed by a government employee, yet being denied any opportunity to seek justice or simply compensation to deal with the consequence. Does that feel like a system "with liberty and justice for all" to you?

When one journalist, Sharyl Attkisson, decided to take on the US Attorney General after the "Justice" Department gained access to her laptop while working at CBS News, she was given a crash course on how immunity sets plaintiffs like her up for failure:

> What's been most striking to me is just how one-sided the rules are when Americans take on their own government… It has been dismaying to learn the extent to which rules and laws shield the government from accountability for its abuses—or even lawbreaking. It's been a long and frightening lesson… The rules seem rigged to protect government lawlessness, and the playing field is uneven. Too many processes favor the government. The deck is still stacked.

Government entities and their employees can now claim immunity for: deeming safe and approving the use of medications or vaccines that harm or kill; using excessive force against innocent people; conducting warrantless searches; searching individuals without reasonable suspicion as is generally required; torturing prisoners; recklessly causing a citizen's death; and much more. In a system where the government is above the law, true justice becomes an illusion, leaving victims to suffer without recourse or remedy.

A World Without It

Doing away with immunity is a cause for concern for many who wonder about the consequences. Wouldn't the government be subject to endless litigation from its citizens? Possibly—but that may create an incentive for the government to involve itself in far fewer aspects of our lives, reducing its footprint so as not to accidentally step on the wrong person. Accountability can be the vehicle for significant political change; just as the DPT manufacturers started to back out when being held accountable, government agencies might boss people around less or be shut down entirely so as to avoid the chance of causing unnecessary harm to others. If each of us is subject to endless lawsuits from people—able to be sued at any time if we cause harm to another—then everyone, including government employees, should be in a similar situation.

In a world without immunity, private companies (pharmaceutical or otherwise) and government employees, such as police officers, would need to carry liability insurance—much like doctors and other professionals do. This insurance would protect them financially in case they were sued for actions taken in the course of duty. However, if an officer were to engage in misconduct, such as using excessive force, or if their agency received multiple complaints about their work, their insurance premiums could then rise given the increased risk. This rise in cost would make it expensive and potentially unsustainable for them to continue in their role, effectively weeding out those who are unfit for the job. Requiring government employees to carry insurance to cover their actions—without an immunity shield—would help weed out bad apples, as insurance companies would be unlikely to provide coverage for problematic people who are too risky to retain.

A system like this would have several positive effects. First, it would create a strong incentive for government employees to act responsibly and ethically, knowing that their actions have direct financial consequences. This accountability would encourage better behavior and also build public trust, as citizens would see that there are real consequences for misconduct. And insurance companies, in an effort to minimize payouts, would serve as an additional layer of oversight, ensuring that claims are thoroughly investigated and addressed.

This financial incentive to investigate problems would also help to dismantle the current culture of impunity and the so-called "blue wall of silence," where police departments or other government agencies often protect their own, even when they have acted inappropriately. Without immunity, there would be greater transparency and a genuine opportunity for justice, as government employees would be held to the same standards as everyone else. This shift would not only improve individual accountability but also lead to broader systemic changes, as departments would have to reconsider their policies and practices to minimize the risk of liability.

A world without immunity laws restores incentives back to where they should have been all along, creating a legal system where bad actors, whether in government or the private sector, can be held accountable. It cultivates a "think twice" approach whereby people pause to consider their actions knowing that they may be personally held responsible for them; just as one is cautious about jumping off a cliff into the lake below, government employees will be incentivized to ensure that their actions don't cause problems before they proceed. It's a system where people are pushed to be on their best behavior. It's a system where "justice for all" is more than a soundbite in a pledge, memorized and regurgitated for children." It's one where "We, the People" can actually hold our own government responsible for its wrongful actions. That's a system where people can actually have an increased measure of freedom.

Tuttle Twins Takeaways

1. Immunity originated from the English monarchy, stating that the king could do no wrong, and was later extended to government entities in the U.S.

2. Immunity protects government employees, like police officers, from being successfully sued for harmful actions performed during their duties, unless they violate "clearly established" laws.

3. Because of immunity, victims are often left without recourse, unable to hold those who harm them accountable in court.

4. Immunity creates a two-tiered justice system, where those protected are not held to the same standards as ordinary citizens, leading to an erosion of public trust.

5. Removing immunity could incentivize better behavior and decision-making, as everyone would face financial and legal consequences for misconduct.

Look, workers! We have saved you from exploitation by the Bourgeoisie!
This feels like the same thing... but worse.
Stop complaining or you will be executed!

MARXISM

Karl Marx's ideas led to widespread suffering, including mass murder, economic collapse, and the suppression of dissent. Are these ideas still influential today?

"A society that puts equality before freedom will get neither. A society that puts freedom before equality will get a high degree of both."

~ Milton Friedman

Karl Marx was born on May 5, 1818, in Trier, a small town in the Kingdom of Prussia (present-day Germany), to a middle-class family. Both of his parents, Heinrich and Henriette, were descended from a long line of Jewish rabbis. Marx's father wanted to be a lawyer, a profession Jews were barred from entering. So he converted to Christianity; young Marx was baptized into the same Lutheran church at age six. Despite the family's religious background and Marx's instruction at a Lutheran elementary school, he would later embrace atheism and attack all religion as "the opium of the people."

Heinrich hoped his son would follow in his footsteps and pursue the practice of law, and, to that end, Marx took several legal courses at the nearby Bonn University. But he was more interested in philosophy and literature than in law. He sought to become a poet and playwright. He studied little and partied a lot, racking up significant debt along the way. Frustrated, his father sent him across the country to the University of Berlin instead. It was a decision that would change the course of world history—for it was in this environment where Marx was exposed to intellectuals who were challenging institutions and ideas across the board. Religion, politics, philosophy, and ethics were all subject to their radical scrutiny. Marx's penchant for questioning authority and established norms began to emerge, even as his academic performance suffered due to his involvement in these groups. But theorizing and philosophizing wouldn't pay the bills, so as Marx graduated, he turned to journalism as a way to support himself.

Some initial setbacks in business led Marx and his new-lywed bride to Paris, a hotbed of radical thinking, where he became editor of a radical periodical called *Rhineland News*; he also collaborated with various revolutionary groups, writing critical essays on politics and philosophy. These thinkers were deeply critical of what they perceived to be the harsh realities of industrial capitalism—poor working conditions, low wages, and hoarding of resources by those who owned the companies. The squalor and exploitation Marx witnessed among the working class profoundly impacted him.

It was here in Paris where he met Friedrich Engels, the son of a wealthy textile manufacturer—an introduction that marked the beginning of a deep intellectual and personal bond. Engels, who had been documenting the harsh realities of the working class in England, and Marx, who was deeply engaged in revolutionary thought, found common ground in their critiques of capitalism and materialist views of history. Their shared interests and perspectives led to a close friendship and collaboration, with Engels providing both intellectual companionship and financial support. That financial support was critical, as Marx was still struggling financially, unable to secure a steady income, and spending the resources he had quite recklessly. His situation was exacerbated by his refusal to compromise his political and philosophical ideals for more lucrative but less meaningful work. Marx's financial difficulties were particularly severe during his time in Paris and later in London. After the *Rhineland News* was shut down by the Prussian government in 1843 due to its radical content, Marx lost his main source of income. His attempts to earn money through journalism and other writing endeavors were sporadic and often poorly compensated. His controversial views and unyielding criticism of established systems made it difficult for him to find publishers willing to take on his work, further limiting his income. This meant his wife and young children were living in extreme poverty conditions. It was Engels' financial contributions that allowed Marx to focus on thinking and writing and activism, providing meager resources for his family to live while he built his revolutionary movement.

This thinking, writing, and activism were laser-focused on improving the plight of the working class. At least, that was the cause they championed publicly; privately, Engels expressed contempt and ridicule for the workers who were serving as their political prop. Still, the perceived exploitation and degradation of laborers in industrialized cities allowed Marx and Engels to portray a stark contrast between the opulent lives of the *bourgeoisie* (middle class) and the comparative squalor endured by the *proletariat* (the working class). They saw capitalism as a system that dehumanized individuals, reducing them to mere cogs in the machinery of profit. Workers were alienated from the fruits of their labor, their toil enriching only a small elite who controlled the means of production. This, Marx argued, was not just an economic injustice but a moral one, as it perpetuated a cycle of oppression and deprivation. He felt that capitalism was not merely an economic framework but a fundamental betrayal of human potential and dignity—a system that had to be overthrown to achieve true freedom and equality.

But to overthrow a system, he needed allies. And in order to recruit allies, he needed a manifesto—a public declaration of his views around which others could rally. So in early 1848, together with Engels, Marx wrote *The Communist Manifesto*.

The Context

As they traveled through and relocated to various parts of Europe, Marx and Engels observed firsthand the consequences of the burgeoning Industrial Revolution. One visible development was the creation of large manufacturing towns, drawing in agricultural workers from surrounding areas hoping for steady, gainful employment no longer tied to the seasonality and whims of weather. The living conditions in these towns were very poor; workers were crowded into slums, and any housing infrastructure was built shoddily. Sanitation was awful, and clean water was scarce. It is little wonder that in such circumstances the death rate would be high: in Manchester, for example, one out of every thirty people died each year; the average age of death was seventeen, compared to thirty-eight in rural areas; and 57 percent of children born to working-class parents died before age five. So it was common for critics at the time to point their ire toward such appalling circumstances; Marx and Engel were certainly not lone voices in decrying the condition of the working class. Their *Communist Manifesto* noted that this wretchedness was a byproduct of the capitalist system, in which the upper classes financially profited from the activities of the worker who "sinks deeper and deeper below the conditions of existence in his own class."

They also observed a longer-term problem—one that they felt would widen the gap between the bourgeoisie and the proletariat. That problem was automation, seen at the time in the decline of handloom weaving. In prior decades, there had been a surge in demand for handloom weavers; by the early 1820s, there were approximately 200,000 of them in Lancashire and Cheshire alone—nearly a quarter of the entire adult male labor force in these counties. And then came the power loom. This device used steam or electricity to more quickly and consistently weave textiles. One person could manage multiple looms, each of which operated at a much higher speed than manual looms. The wages of handloom weavers plummeted, and by the time *The Communist Manifesto* came onto the scene, these weavers were among the most poverty-stricken workers in England. "The increasing improvement of machinery," Marx wrote, "ever more rapidly developing, makes [workers'] livelihood more and more precarious." Not only were they "slaves of the bourgeois class"; as a result of technology and the advances of the Industrial Revolution, workers were, in Marx's view, "enslaved by the machine."

But beyond poor conditions and the threat of technology to workers, Marx directed his attacks to the foundation of the capitalist economy itself—one that he argued led to the concentration of wealth and power in the hands of a few, exacerbating inequality and societal instability. Marx contended that capitalism commodified everything, including human labor, reducing workers to mere instruments of production whose value was determined solely by their ability to generate profit. Workers in this system were forced to "sell themselves piecemeal," he wrote; they "live only so long as they find work, and... find work only so long as their labor increases capital" to enrich the bourgeoisie. As a result, workers were "exposed to all the vicissitudes of competition, to all the fluctuations of the market."

So this was the diagnosis. Capitalism was evil, employers were taking advantage of workers, technology was a threat, and the system was corrupt to its core. But a diagnosis is just an opinion until there's action—a proposed solution to remedy the problem. What did Marx say should be done to resolve his ceaseless complaints? As he wrote in his manifesto, "The theory of the Communists may be summed up in a single sentence: abolition of private property." Marx and Engels believed that land should be collectively owned and managed to benefit society as a whole—and that private property ownership was the bedrock of the capitalist system; if the bourgeoisie could not own their assets—if those assets were required to be redistributed to benefit everyone—then they could not build an enterprise that enriched them at others' expense. But *The Communist Manifesto* didn't stop there. Marx also proposed, among other ideas:

- A heavy income tax where the wealthy would pay a higher percentage of their income in taxes in order to reduce income inequality.

- Abolishing all rights of inheritance to prevent the accumulation of wealth within particular families or classes.

- Confiscating the property of immigrants and those who opposed the communists.

- Creating a national bank so the state could control the financial system, including credit and currency, to ensure that economic resources would be used in the public interest rather than for private profit.

- Distributing labor across the entire population by creating an equal liability for everyone to work, potentially in state-organized industrial armies.

- Offering "free education" for all children in state-operated schools in order to "rescue education from the influence of the ruling class."

"The Communists disdain to conceal their views and aims," Marx wrote in the concluding paragraph of the book. "They openly declare that their ends can be attained only by the forcible overthrow of all existing social conditions. Let the ruling classes tremble at a Communistic revolution. The proletarians have nothing to lose but their chains. They have a world to win." He believed that only by abolishing the capitalist system and restructuring society on socialist principles could humanity achieve true freedom, equality, and justice. Communism was more than a set of revolutionary ideas—it was Marx's utopian dream.

Why is it the Worst Idea?

In reality, it was a nightmare.

After decades of being attacked, censored, and oppressed, the communists got a toehold in Russia after the October Revolution—a coup in late 1917 by a group of socialists organized by Vladimir Lenin, a self-avowed Marxist. Following a civil war lasting five years, Lenin's comrades prevailed and created the Soviet Union in late 1922—the world's first communist state. And their revolutionary fervor radiated to other countries, where communist parties were formed to agitate as well. But the promise of a classless, stateless society quickly gave way to a brutal and oppressive regime. The Soviet Union, under Lenin and later Joseph Stalin, became a symbol of the horrors of communism in practice. The state tightly controlled all aspects of life, eliminating political dissent, suppressing free speech, and implementing severe censorship. The collectivization of agriculture led to widespread famine, most notably the Holodomor in Ukraine, where millions perished due to starvation and forced grain requisitions. The government's ruthless policies also included purges, forced labor camps (Gulags), and mass executions, targeting anyone perceived as a threat to the state or the Communist Party's ideology.

In China, Mao Zedong's Great Leap Forward and Cultural Revolution resulted in tens of millions of deaths due to famine, forced labor, and political persecution. Similarly, in Cambodia, Pol Pot's Khmer Rouge regime sought to create an agrarian utopia, leading to the genocide of approximately a quarter of the population. These atrocities illustrate the horrific flaws in communist ideology, where the concentration of power in the hands of the state leads to widespread abuse by those in power who suppress individual freedoms. The pursuit of an idealized, egalitarian society often resulted in catastrophic human suffering, economic collapse, and the stifling of innovation and personal initiative.

While communism seemed utopian and altruistic on paper, reality was vastly different. It's one thing to write provocative, even crazy, ideas. It's another to put them into practice and see their inevitable consequences play out. As the power of the state was used to eradicate class distinctions in communist societies, they also lost their humanity. Workers became slaves, working under inhuman conditions. And yet, there remained two classes: those in power and everyone else. The history of communism is indisputably shocking: tens of millions of people died in communist countries, purged by their own governments, in the name of reshaping society and creating a better world for workers. Beyond those who died as a direct result of Marx's ideas, countless millions more starved, became sick, were displaced, and otherwise suffered.

Naturally, people turned against the revolutionaries; the communists were far more brutal than the rulers they replaced. And private property owners didn't take kindly to the state seizing their assets. So, unsurprisingly, communist regimes frequently resorted to extreme measures to maintain control and enforce conformity. The use of secret police, widespread surveillance, and a culture of fear ensured that dissent was quickly silenced. In Eastern Europe, satellite states under Soviet influence experienced similar repression, with uprisings in Hungary and Czechoslovakia brutally crushed. The Berlin Wall became a stark symbol of the communist state's willingness to imprison its own citizens to prevent them from fleeing to the West. The communist movement's adopted emblem, the hammer and the sickle, originally symbolized industry and agriculture. At least for the hammer, it soon came to represent the crushing totalitarianism of those who wielded it.

Sadly, communism is not entirely a thing of the past. At one point, nearly one-third of the entire world's population lived in communist states; the fall of the Berlin Wall and a series of revolutions in 1989 resulted in the collapse of most Marxist governments. Yet, some remain: North Korea, China, Cuba, Laos, and Vietnam all operate under one-party Marxist-Leninist rule. From the perspective of those who govern in these countries, they are not actually communist—rather, they are socialist states that are in the process of progressing toward a communist society. It is an ideal toward which they claim to strive. And in the process, like all communist states before them, the citizens suffer under oppressive regimes that control the economy, suppress dissent, and restrict basic freedoms like speech, worship, association, self-defense, travel, and more.

But Marxism has not remained confined to these few countries; like a virus, it has adapted to its new environment, mutating to more easily be able to replicate itself by successfully bypassing its host's defenses. When Marx and Engels wrote *The Communist Manifesto*, their chief concern was with private property ownership—the foundation of the capitalist system. Their successors have adapted or expanded Marxism beyond mere economic concerns; today's mutation is called cultural Marxism. Remember that the communists' concern was the existence of classes: many who were oppressed by the few oppressors—the haves and the have-nots. Cultural Marxists take this same concept and apply it to a host of other things: schools, families, churches, sports, and more. Everywhere they look, communists today—even if they don't call themselves that—see unfairness and "income inequality." They look with jealousy to those who have built up enterprise, and instead of simply objecting to their private ownership of property, they object to every part of the culture that has let someone with "privilege" rise above others. Like crabs in a bucket, they want to pull down anyone who climbs above them. They don't just want to abolish private property—they want to dismantle anything in society that makes some more successful than others. Their dream is not equality of opportunity—where everyone is free to pursue their dreams and work hard to create a successful life—but rather equity, where the "underprivileged" are artificially supported through reparations, subsidies, priority benefits, and more to ensure they can obtain the same outcomes as others. It is communism on a far greater scale—not the Marxist monster many are used to, but a multi-headed hydra known by Critical Race Theory, or "Diversity, Equity, and Inclusion," or affirmative action, or social justice, or equity.

Communism didn't collapse. It evolved. Many millions of people have died and suffered as a result of Marx's dystopian dreams. Many more will be harmed if this virus is not contained.

A World Without It

Four years prior to helping Marx write and publish *The Communist Manifesto*, Engels wrote a book titled *The Condition of the Working Class in England*. His report of workers' warfare was based on data from Parliament's politically-motivated investigations into the Industrial Revolution, with information supplied by people who wanted to validate the anti-market sentiments of those in power. Far from being an exhaustive, neutral review of the data, it was a skewed set of findings meant to reinforce the establishment perspective that the economic changes underway were a threat to the existing order. No wonder Marx, Engels, and others were so quick to capitalize on horror stories of workers' conditions when that's what the official narrative popularized.

As a modern counterpart, consider a Congressional investigation of alleged sweatshop conditions in factories. Those selected to testify would no doubt be people who would share cherry-picked horror stories—the worst examples that can be found. Chances are, the committee tasked with investigating this issue would not pause to question why these workers were voluntarily choosing to work in so-called "sweatshops" when they could be enjoying life in the countryside, free from the demands of urban industrialization. Even in Marx's era, workers' lives were being improved by the changing economy. The Industrial Revolution did not result in the poor getting poorer and the rich getting richer as a result of the perceived oppression of capitalists. In fact, everyone's standard of living increased because of innovation, technological advancements, and the division of labor. This is why people voluntarily fled the countryside; rural life was more difficult, dangerous, and unpredictable.

Put simply: the observations that Marx and Engels made—the "problems" they perceived for which they offered communism as a solution—were totally incorrect. Workers were not being oppressed and exploited. They were slowly improving their lives by voluntarily choosing opportunities that might help them accumulate wealth over time. Sure, there were risks—but there were plenty of other risks remaining on the family farm trying to eke out a living at the mercy of the elements. So because Marx's ideas did not actually improve the condition of workers, we need not struggle to imagine what a world without them would be like. Prosperity around the world—even for the poorest of the poor—has increased not due to anything related to communism but in spite of it. The same economic progress that was already underway because of the Industrial Revolution has continued in recent years; technology, automation, and continued industrialization have created an abundance of wealth and opportunity far greater than Marx could have dreamed.

Except his dream wasn't ultimately about wealth for workers—it was to use them as a political prop to advance his agenda. That agenda is carried on today by the cultural Marxists, whose ideas have infected institutions across society: corporations, news media, universities, churches, nonprofits, and more. Everywhere around us are people wanting to "dismantle the system" because they perceive that it unfairly rewards some people (not including them) and perpetuates injustice for which they champion "equity" (or, communism) as the solution. Imagine that this virus was eradicated through the invention of a new pill people could take to inoculate themselves against the infection; society would be free of this diseased perspective and instead allow innovators, hard workers, and talented people to achieve more than the rest of us. We would see a greater emphasis on individual merit, personal responsibility, and the free exchange of ideas and goods. The absence of a narrative that pits groups against each other based on identity or class would allow for a more harmonious society where people are encouraged to excel based on their abilities and efforts. The focus would shift from dismantling existing systems to improving them, ensuring that everyone has the opportunity to succeed based on their own circumstances, abilities, and desires.

Of course, a world without Marxism means millions upon millions of people would be alive today who were killed by communist states. It would also mean that those living under the remaining communist states today would be liberated, able to enjoy essential freedoms and improved economic conditions to better their lives. And, importantly, society would recognize and reward merit, progress, and achievement, furthering the innovation and productivity of humanity instead of suppressing success in the name of propping up those who fall behind. Society's institutions would be stronger and would reinforce this cultural attitude instead of being hollowed out from within by activists looking to use the institution's resources and influence to further cultural Marxism's goals.

Workers, the "underprivileged," and the "oppressed"— the intended beneficiaries of economic Marxism and its cultural variants—would no longer be political props for communist would-be dictators looking to leverage their plight to consolidate power. Instead, we would have a free economy that would improve everyone's lives—an economic rising tide that lifts all boats, regardless of size or status. Because Marxists would no longer be arbitrarily redistributing resources, capital would flow toward its most productive use; innovators would be incentivized to start companies, create new products and services, and, in the process, create good-paying jobs and opportunities for everyone else. This environment would foster a culture of excellence, where success is celebrated and merit is the primary criterion for advancement. The result would be a more dynamic economy, characterized by high productivity, technological advancements, and improved standards of living for all.

Finally, a society free from the divisive narratives of cultural Marxism would be more cohesive and united. Without the constant emphasis on group identity and systemic oppression, people would be more likely to see each other as individuals with unique talents and perspectives—not as members of a group saddled with its associated stereotypes. This shift would promote greater social harmony—a culture of mutual respect and understanding where individuals are judged by their character and abilities rather than preconceived notions and biased perspectives.

In essence, a world without Marxism and its viral variants would be one where human potential can be fully realized. It would be a world where individuals are free to pursue their dreams, where merit and effort are rewarded, and where the benefits of economic growth and innovation are widely shared. Society would be founded on cooperation and competition, not coercion; we could each pursue a better life without having to take resources from others, building our success without undermining theirs.

Tuttle Twins Takeaways

1. Marx and Engels viewed capitalism as a system that exploited and dehumanized workers, concentrating wealth among a few elites.

2. *The Communist Manifesto* advocated for the abolition of private property and proposed radical reforms to dismantle capitalist structures.

3. The implementation of communism in various countries led to mass murder, stifling of dissent, economic failures, and widespread suffering.

4. Modern Marxist ideologies have evolved into cultural Marxism, infiltrating various societal institutions and promoting divisive narratives.

5. Marxist ideologies suppress individual merit and innovation, instead aiming to control the economy in order to forcibly redistribute resources to the underprivileged and oppressed.

It's very suspicious for a woman to be carrying around so much money. I'm placing this cash under arrest!
...but, I was just on my way to buy a new car. That's all I have.
Tell it to the judge!

CIVIL ASSET FORFEITURE

In the name of fighting crime, law enforcement officials are financially incentivized to take property from innocent people without due process.

"When plunder becomes a way of life for a group of men in a society, over time they create for themselves a legal system that authorizes it and a moral code that glorifies it."

~ Frederic Bastiat

In the golden age of British naval dominance, the seas were a vast and often lawless frontier. The British Empire, with its formidable navy, held a tight grip on maritime trade routes and sought to protect its commercial interests from the threats of piracy, smuggling, and rival nations. To help maintain order and assert control, the Crown developed a comprehensive legal framework that allowed for the seizure of vessels and their cargoes, a practice known as prize law, which targeted not only enemy ships during times of war but also those engaged in illicit activities. By confiscating the assets of those who violated these laws, the British authorities aimed to deter criminal behavior on the high seas and assert their supremacy, ensuring the safe passage of goods and wealth that fueled the empire's global ambitions.

The legal process around seizing ships and their assets was not that simple, however; typically, a government that follows due process must charge and convict a person with a crime prior to confiscating his belongings. This is an *in personem* legal proceeding (Latin for "against the person")—one in which the government must locate a person and have jurisdiction over them in court. But the ship's owners were often located in a different part of the world than the seized ships themselves, necessitating a different kind of proceeding, one called *in rem* (Latin for "against a thing")—where the court takes action not against a person but against a piece of property. Now courts could transfer legal ownership over seized assets with relative ease, something that the government found convenient and lucrative amid a growing mercantile industry.

Across the pond, American colonists modeled their laws after the Crown's; the first U.S. Congress used this template to create the country's first forfeiture statutes in order to collect customs duties. Like their mother country, they found it a convenient, expedited way in which to pursue claims against owners who were located elsewhere in the world and thus beyond the reach of U.S. courts. Enforcing customs laws—the import and export of goods—remained the primary focus for forfeiture laws for a century, until war between the states broke out. The US government used this process to confiscate the property both of Southern rebels as well as their sympathizers. Congress passed the Confiscation Act on July 17, 1862, authorizing *in rem* court proceedings against rebel property. And when challenged, it was upheld by the US Supreme Court as an inherent power of the government in wartime:

> The power to declare war involves the power to prosecute it by all means and in any manner in which war may be legitimately prosecuted. It therefore includes the right to seize and confiscate all property of the enemy and dispose of it at the will of the captor.

This, of course, was applied to enemies of the state—those they claimed to be traitors who were not afforded the protection of the very laws against which they were rebelling. It is important to note this distinction: forfeiture laws were not used against citizens who were afforded constitutional protections before being separated from their property. That trend didn't last long, as a few decades later, Congress declared a new war in which forfeiture would play a key role—a war on liquor as part of the Prohibition era from 1919 to 1933. Those who violated the Volstead Act, which outlawed the production, importation, and distribution of most alcoholic beverages, could have their property confiscated if caught. In one case, an auto dealer leased some vehicles to people who then used them to transport illegal liquor. Once caught, their vehicles were seized by the government using the law that allowed them to forfeit property used in the illegal transportation of alcohol. Despite the owner of the vehicles—the auto dealership—having no involvement or even any knowledge that the vehicles would be used this way, the US Supreme Court ruled the forfeiture was constitutional, even if the owner was innocent and unaware of the illegal use. Why? Because the government was taking action *in rem*—against a piece of property—and not against its owner. They, therefore, argued that the owner's involvement or knowledge wasn't required in order to take action against the vehicles themselves.

The thinking behind forfeiture is that a piece of property does not share the rights of a person. When the property is the focus of a court action, there's no right to an attorney and, in most jurisdictions, no presumption of innocence. But it's important to note that there are actually two types of forfeiture: *criminal* asset forfeiture and *civil* asset forfeiture. The former is what you would expect from a government that protects its citizens' rights; property can only be taken as part of a criminal proceeding, in which a person is charged with a crime and convicted by (if he so chooses) a jury of his peers. It makes sense, for example, that a person who stole money from a bank should, if convicted, be deprived of using the ill-gotten gains anymore; criminals who violate the law can have their property taken if convicted. This makes sense. What makes far less sense—and has become far more common—is the latter type: civil asset forfeiture. This is where *in rem* comes into play. The government doesn't need to convict anyone, as in the case of the car dealer during Prohibition. The property has no rights, and prosecutors can avoid protracted criminal trials where they have to establish enough evidence to obtain a conviction against the accused. Thus, in civil asset forfeiture, the defendant is the asset itself. This leads to court cases like *United States v. One Pearl Necklace* and *United States v. Approximately 64,695 Pounds of Shark Fins* or *The State of Texas v. Five Thousand Dollars in Cash*.

The Context

As the Prohibition era thankfully faded into history, a new front in the fight against illicit substances emerged: the war on drugs. This campaign, starting in the 1970s, brought with it a significant expansion of civil asset forfeiture laws. Under a series of laws passed over a decade and a half, Congress made civil forfeiture become a central component in the fight against drug trafficking and crime more generally. The law stated that law enforcement agencies could forfeit "all real property... which is used, or intended to be used, in any manner or part, to commit, or to facilitate the commission of... a violation." In plain English, this said that if police believed your money or car or computer or house or anything else was used in furtherance of a crime—or if it was the results of a crime, like money stolen from a bank—then the government could take it.

This expansion of forfeiture laws radically increased their abuse by police agencies, targeting people to take their property. Out of the many thousands of stories that might be shared, consider Jennifer Boatright, a waitress from

Houston. With her two children and her boyfriend, she drove toward Linden, her boyfriend's home town, to visit his father as they did each April. This time, they planned to buy a used car while there, so they brought some cash along with them. The travelers were soon pulled over by a police officer, though they were not speeding or breaking any law. He asked if they had any drugs, and they replied no. The officer then asked for permission to search the car, and, knowing they had nothing illegal, they consented. The officer found the cash and took it. In the police report, the officer said that Boatright and her boyfriend fit the profile of drug couriers because they were driving from Houston, "a known point for distribution of illegal narcotics," to Linden, "a known place to receive illegal narcotics." The report said that the children were possible decoys, meant to distract police.

Now escorted to the police station—despite not being arrested or charged with a crime—the couple were introduced to the district attorney, who told them that they could face felony charges for money laundering and child endangerment, risking jail time and having the children placed in foster care. Or, the attorney said, they could relinquish their claims to the cash, letting law enforcement keep it, and then get back on the road. "Where are we?" Boatright recalls thinking. "Is this some kind of foreign country…?"

Police and prosecutors justify their widespread use of civil asset forfeiture by arguing that they are important tools to fight powerful drug cartels; by seizing the money they make from drug sales and the property they use to facilitate their crimes, they can be economically weakened. (Or so the theory goes.) But in practice, forfeiture laws extend far beyond drug kingpins and traffickers to include small-time offenders and completely innocent people. Since the war on drugs began and forfeiture laws were expanded, they have been introduced into more than 400 federal statutes and hundreds of state laws around the country. The legal tool, once rarely used and only on foreigners and traitors, has now turned inward to be applied to hundreds of thousands, if not millions, of American citizens. In fact, a *Washington Post* investigation in 2014 found that federal law enforcement officers were taking more property from people, using civil asset forfeiture, than burglars did; over $5 billion was seized using forfeiture whereas, according to the FBI, some $3.5 billion was stolen by thieves.

Boatright's situation is by no means an isolated incident—it's a symptom of a broader issue affecting many Americans. Across the country, individuals have found themselves stripped of their property without even being charged with a crime. In many instances, the mere presence of cash, without any other evidence of illegal activity, has been sufficient grounds for forfeiture. This appalling abuse has thankfully led to widespread criticism and calls for reform of a system that currently prioritizes financial gain over justice and due process. The overarching impact of civil asset forfeiture has been a chilling effect on individual rights—particularly property rights—with many left wondering if they could have their possessions taken by the government simply by being in the wrong place at the wrong time. The war on drugs, supposedly crafted to target powerful cartels, has instead ensnared countless ordinary Americans in a legal quagmire, where their rights to due process and property are increasingly overshadowed by the profit motives of law enforcement agencies.

Why is it the Worst Idea?

Tony Jalali fled from Iran in 1978 and emigrated to the US, looking forward to living under a legal system that respected the rule of law, due process, and individual freedom. Stepping foot onto American soil, he never could've imagined that the government in which he placed his hope would one day try to steal everything he had built. Over the years, he scrimped and saved, finally investing his family's life savings into a small office building in Anaheim, California, with multiple tenants. One of his renters was a medical cannabis dispensary—legal under state law but in violation of federal law, which continued to prohibit cannabis as part of the overall war on drugs. Jalali had never run afoul of the law, yet the police opened a forfeiture case against him because of the dispensary—this despite neither Jalali nor his tenants even being charged with the crime. Prosecutors tried to take away his entire $1.5 million commercial building—home also to a dentist, an insurance company, and the business office of a car dealer.

Why would the police come after Jalali and his entire building? The profit motive previously mentioned is why; police and prosecutors are financially incentivized to take people's property. To understand this better, we need to explore the case a bit more—because it wasn't just the police that were involved. They had teamed up with federal officials; police would investigate and seize assets, and then the case would be transferred to federal prosecutors, who would pursue the forfeiture case in federal court. The reason for this arrangement is a heavy financial incentive for police that seize property: if they hand the case over to the feds and they successfully forfeit the property, then the local police can receive up to 80 percent of the property's value—a huge payout for doing hardly any of the work. Motivated police officers across the country now have a revenue stream to buy additional tools and toys behind their limited budgets approved by the city council. These funds have been used by law enforcement agencies to increase salaries, pay bonuses, and buy equipment—ranging from the arguably excessive (helicopters and armored personnel carriers) to the absurd (margarita machines). In Tulsa, Oklahoma, officers drove around in a Cadillac Escalade they had taken through forfeiture, now featuring the stenciled words, "This Used To Be a Drug Dealer's Car, Now It's Ours!"

This system creates a perverse incentive for agencies to prioritize financial gain over justice. In Jalali's case, the local police were motivated to seize his property, not because of the severity of any crime but because of the potential financial windfall. Under the guise of combating drug-related crime, they targeted a law-abiding property owner simply because one of his tenants was involved in a business that, while legal under state law, conflicted with federal regulations. Across the country, over 8,000 police agencies reacting to these heavy financial incentives receive a total of nearly half a billion dollars each year. And the gravy train flows as well as it does because forfeiture laws are more favorable to prosecutors trying to take property; many states have enacted tougher laws to clamp down on the process, so police instead find creative ways to involve their federal partners to circumvent these citizen protections and still seize the property.

Jalali would have lost his life savings were it not for the Institute for Justice, a legal firm that offered to help for free. It took two years of lawsuits and headaches, but he prevailed and was able to keep his property. His case has a happy ending, whereas the overwhelming majority of cases do not. And part of the reason is that seizing a $1.5 million asset is rare; if your family's home was taken, for example, you and relatives and friends would band together to hire a lawyer and fight the government; you would be financially incentivized to spend, say, $25,000 on lawyer fees, in the hopes of retaining a $1 million home.

But most forfeitures fall far below that amount. In most states, the average amount seized is $1–3,000; in Washington, DC, the average is under $200. Now consider: would you hire that same lawyer and spend $25,000 on legal fees, in the hopes of recovering a thousand bucks? Clearly not. In this case, you would be financially incentivized to leave the property alone and let police and prosecutors get away with it. Owners whose property is seized often find that the cost of hiring a lawyer far exceeds the value of the property. It just doesn't make sense to put up a fight, so most don't.

One review of federal forfeitures found that property owners challenged the seizures only in one-sixth of cases—16 percent! And interestingly, when property owners fought back legally, the government agreed to return money in 41 percent of cases. In many of the cases, to get their property back, the owners were first required to sign agreements saying they would not sue the police. It may sound great that nearly half of property owners who fought back received money, and it's certainly better than losing your property entirely. The reality is that the total amount is very rarely returned. Typically what happens is that you hire a lawyer, and prosecutors see that it will be a hassle to deal with this case, so they offer a deal: you keep half, they keep half, the lawsuit ends, and both parties walk away—split the baby and move on. So your lawyer presents the offer and counsels you to take it. Again, better to get something than nothing—or spend even more on legal fees on the risk that you fail. Not only does the government keep most of the property it seizes because the amount is often too low for people to justify hiring an attorney, but it also retains a substantial amount of property, even when people fight back. They win; you lose.

Civil asset forfeiture is a horrible idea born out of the British Empire and its insatiable desire for naval dominance. It has evolved over time in America into a systematized way in which law enforcement officials abuse the citizens whose rights they are supposed to protect. These laws perpetuate a profound injustice that subverts the very principles of due process and property rights. They empower the government to seize assets without charging individuals with a crime, placing the burden of proof on property owners to reclaim what is rightfully theirs. Civil asset forfeiture not only erodes public trust in law enforcement but also incentivizes policing for profit rather than justice. It is, in short, legalized theft.

A World Without It

The more people learn about civil asset forfeiture, the less they like it. One public opinion poll revealed that 59 percent of Americans oppose "allowing law enforcement agencies to use forfeited property or its proceeds for their own use." By contrast, only 22 percent said they support the practice—an almost 3-to-1 margin. And when asked about the equitable sharing financial incentive, 70 percent of respondents opposed the program. This growing opposition has led to political reform across the country, with more than half of all US states passing some form of asset forfeiture reform. These legal changes include: requiring data reporting to allow investigators and the public to see how often forfeiture is happening; requiring a conviction in criminal court before prosecutors can seize property through the civil process; shifting the burden of proof so the government has to prove in court that a property owner is guilty of a crime; and limiting the use of funds derived from forfeiture and removing the financial incentive by not allowing cities and their law enforcement agencies to receive the revenue.

Beyond these legal tweaks, a few states have gone further to completely end the practice. New Mexico was the first state to do so in 2015—the result of legislation that passed unanimously. But it wasn't without opposition; by the way the law enforcement community responded, you might have assumed they were dealing with a "defund the police" movement looking to abolish law enforcement altogether. The New Mexico Department of Public Safety claimed that eliminating civil asset forfeiture would have "a negative impact on public safety," and could trigger a "reduction in criminal investigations." The legislation, they said, "directly jeopardizes the most basic and fundamental key to successful narcotics investigations." The chair of the New Mexico Sheriff's Association was more direct, arguing that "you'll get less law enforcement" without civil forfeiture.

"The end result of this," he said, "is the cartels are going to ramp up their money laundering and cash exchanges in the state of New Mexico tenfold."

It's an interesting prediction—and one that can be investigated now that many years have passed. Did drug-related crime increase *tenfold*—or to any degree—in the wake of abolishing civil asset forfeiture? A study in 2020 by the Institute for Justice, five years after the change, "detected no significant increase in crime rates that could be attributed to the reforms, indicating the reforms had no negative effect on public safety—and strongly suggesting civil forfeiture is not an essential crime-fighting tool." The study's authors looked at crime and arrest data before and after the practice was stopped—specifically, they looked at all crimes committed, all arrests, DUI arrests, drug possession arrests, and arrests for selling drugs. Crime didn't increase, nor was there "less law enforcement" because officers had fewer financial resources. What did change was that innocent citizens were able to keep their resources because their police and prosecutorial predators had been defanged. There was, of course, another change. Prior to abolishing civil asset forfeiture, law enforcement agencies in New Mexico were entitled to keep 100 percent of the resulting revenue under state law, as well as the equitable sharing funds from the federal government—millions of dollars per year. (No wonder they opposed the bill that stopped this self-serving flow of cash.)

The experience in New Mexico serves as a crucial lesson: ending civil asset forfeiture does not lead to a collapse in law enforcement effectiveness or public safety. Instead, it offers a model for how police can operate without the perverse incentives that come from seizing citizens' property for profit. By removing the financial motivation behind civil forfeiture, New Mexico has demonstrated that law enforcement can prioritize justice over revenue generation. This shift not only protects the rights of innocent individuals but also keeps law enforcement focused on investigating crime instead of chasing cash. As more states consider reforming or abolishing civil asset forfeiture, the lessons from New Mexico provide a compelling case for why this practice should be ended. It reaffirms the principle that in a free society, the government should not have the unchecked power to take property without due process and that true public safety is best achieved through respect for individual rights.

Tuttle Twins Takeaways

1. Civil asset forfeiture originated from British maritime law which allowed the seizure of enemy ships and smuggler vessels.

2. The American legal system adopted similar forfeiture laws, initially to enforce customs duties and later to confiscate property from Southern rebels during the Civil War.

3. During Prohibition, civil asset forfeiture expanded to include the seizure of property used in the illegal transportation of alcohol. The war on drugs in the 1970s and 1980s further expanded civil asset forfeiture, enabling the seizure of property believed to be connected to drug crimes. This expansion has led to widespread abuse and targeting of innocent individuals.

4. Law enforcement agencies benefit financially from civil forfeiture, creating a profit motive that can undermine justice. This system incentivizes the seizure of property, even in cases involving minor offenses or innocent individuals.

5. Civil asset forfeiture is fundamentally unjust, violating due process and property rights. True public safety is achieved by upholding these principles rather than through the unchecked power of civil forfeiture.

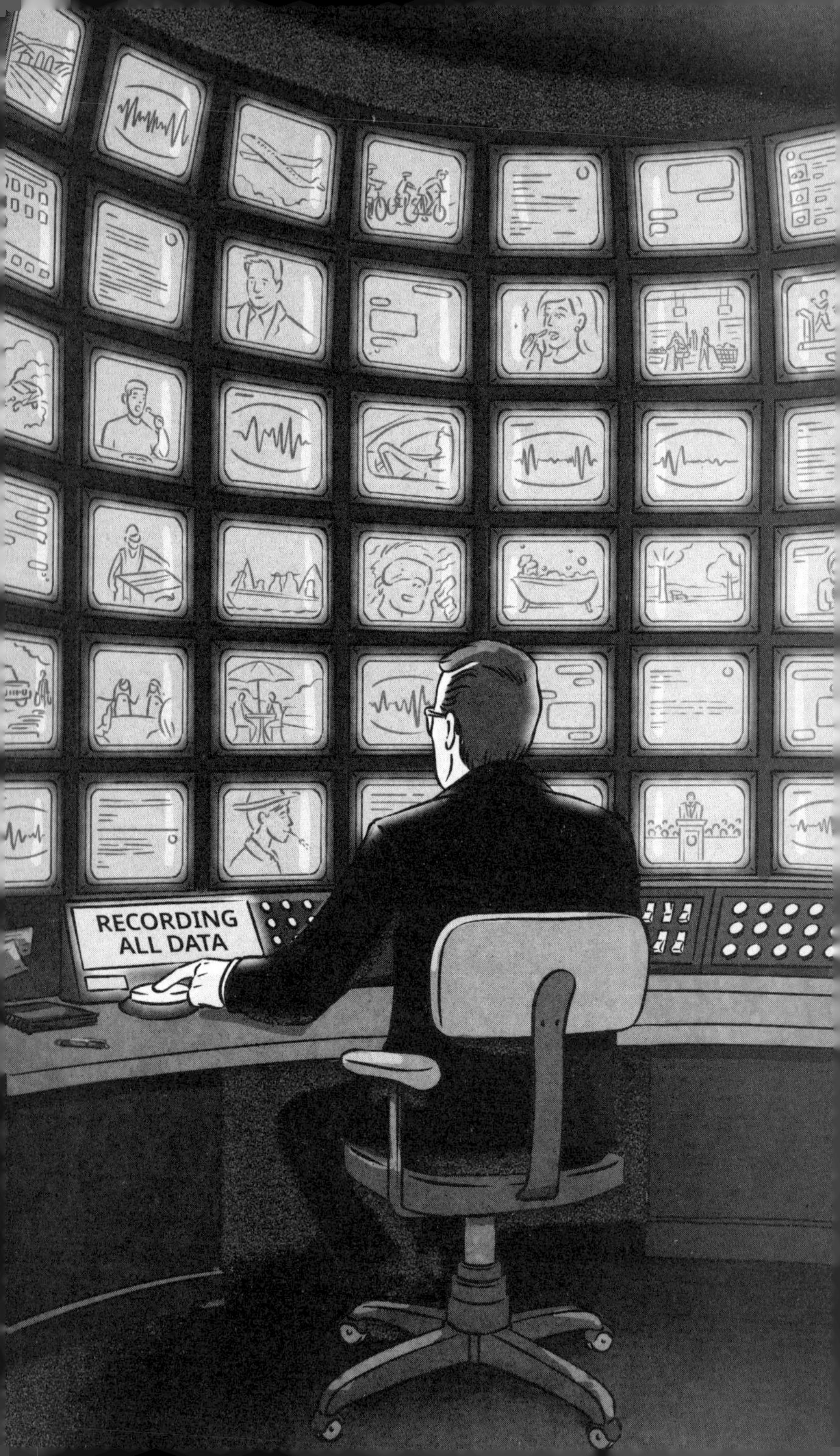
RECORDING
ALL DATA

PERMANENT RECORD

In the wake of 9/11, the government expanded its surveillance systems to catalog everyone's digital activity, creating an Orwellian database to monitor your online activity.

"The permanent record isn't about something you did wrong, it's about something you might want to do in the future."

~ Edward Snowden

Fresh out of a decade-long sentence in the Indiana State Prison for stealing $50 from a grocery store (about $1,000 today) and assaulting someone while trying to flee, John Dillinger was restored to freedom. In prison, he had befriended multiple convicts, and together they planned various heists they would execute. But his buddies were still behind bars, and Dillinger needed a way to accelerate their release. He decided that bribing prison guards would work best and needed to find some fast cash to make it happen. So he paid a visit to the New Carlisle National Bank on June 21, 1933—not to withdraw money from his account but to steal what he needed from its vault. Three employees were held under gunpoint by a couple accomplices Dillinger brought along, tied with telephone wire, while he scooped up silver and banknotes worth over $10,000 (or around $250,000 today).

Over the next year, Dillinger and his associates would rob a dozen banks, killing ten people and wounding seven more. They also robbed police arsenals in multiple cities, stealing machine guns, rifles, revolvers, ammunition, and several bulletproof vests. The group evaded police in four states, and Dillinger himself went to great lengths to evade detection. At one point, he paid a doctor to erase his fingerprints; the physician cut away the outer layer of skin, scraped away at the remaining visible ridges, and then treated Dillinger's fingertips with hydrochloric acid.

He wasn't quite successful—the fingertips grew back mostly intact—but Dillinger was on to something. In the years prior, fingerprint tracking had revolutionized criminal investigations by providing a reliable method of identifying individuals based on unique physical traits. This innovation significantly enhanced law enforcement's ability to solve crimes by linking suspects to crime scenes with unprecedented accuracy. It marked a critical shift from reliance on witness testimony and circumstantial evidence to a more scientific approach. And that's precisely what J. Edgar Hoover wanted.

Hoover was a longtime employee of the Bureau of Investigation—a group of federal law enforcement officials, though small in number and with not much power. At the time, crime was largely a local matter; federal officials had few laws they were required to directly enforce. But Hoover envisioned a far more professional and robust law enforcement agency in the federal government. In 1924, he created the Identification Division to gather fingerprints from police agencies across the country, centralizing access to this important information. It was a landmark development in creating databases with information on citizens that the government could access—a permanent record of people's personally identifiable information. Now serving as director of the Bureau, Hoover turned his team into a national hub for crime records.

Dillinger's multi-state crime spree helped Hoover consolidate power and turn the Bureau of Investigation (BOI) into the Federal Bureau of Investigation (FBI)—a much larger and better-funded version of its smaller past self. The agency developed more sophisticated investigative and surveillance techniques to target criminals, yet these tools would later be used to target political adversaries and innocent individuals as well. As revolutionary as their tactics were for the time, they were still limited because of their analog nature; compiling paper records and maintaining file systems was an inefficient and ineffective way to monitor criminal activity and identify culprits. Criminal records, fingerprints, and other crucial information were stored on paper, often in disparate locations. This meant that sharing information across state lines or even between neighboring counties required physical transfers of documents, a slow and cumbersome process prone to errors and delays. Consequently, criminals could slip through the cracks, as law enforcement agencies struggled to keep track of them in real time.

Bank robbers like Dillinger, serial murderers, fraudsters, and more could often get away with their crimes by moving from one city to the next. Local police departments often operated in isolation, with limited communication and cooperation across jurisdictions. This disjointed approach made it relatively easy for criminals to exploit gaps in the system, moving from one place to another to evade capture. That wasn't for lack of effort; Hoover and his team employed a variety of surveillance techniques to tackle organized crime. Stakeouts, wiretaps, and informant networks were primary methods of gathering intelligence. These methods required significant manpower and were often inefficient. Surveillance teams could only be in one place at a time, and without modern tracking technologies, following a suspect was fraught with difficulties. Criminals with the resources to change their appearances (or try and destroy their fingerprints), use aliases, or simply move frequently could easily outmaneuver law enforcement.

The Context

Society's adoption of digital technologies provided an opening to vastly expand the scope of surveillance and build a permanent record of citizens' activities, whereabouts, and communications. That task largely fell to the National Security Agency (NSA), founded in 1952 to initially decipher foreign communications during the Cold War. Over time, its mission expanded to include extensive domestic surveillance, especially following the attacks on September 11, 2001. Unlike paper-based past methods, digital surveillance enables the NSA to collect a wide range of information, including phone calls, emails, text messages, and internet activity. This data collection is not limited only to foreign enemies or citizens suspected of criminal activity; instead, it encompasses virtually everyone, creating a comprehensive record of personal information—a host of data points about each person far more revealing and informative than mere fingerprints.

As you might imagine, the existence of this surveillance system was highly classified; the government built a "Big Brother" machine and wanted no one to know. In fact, they benefited from the secrecy, for if someone knows they're being monitored, they might go to greater lengths to conceal their private information. But the secret went public when Edward Snowden, an NSA contractor working in Hawaii, blew the whistle and provided reporters with access to a treasure trove of confidential documents explaining the lengths to which the government had gone to surveil its own citizens. As Snowden explained, he had "practically unlimited access to the communications of nearly every man, woman, and child on earth who'd ever dialed a phone or touched a computer." He felt so concerned about the violation of people's privacy that he decided an exposé was required so that people were informed about what their government was doing.

The documents Snowden shared revealed programs like PRISM and XKeyscore, which empowered the NSA to access private communications and track the online activities of millions of people. The NSA could monitor phone metadata, email content, browsing histories, and even social media interactions, all without individual warrants authorizing the invasion of each person's privacy. This information was stored indefinitely, forming a detailed and permanent record of each person's digital footprint. Unlike the fragmented and often incomplete records of the analog era, digital data is comprehensive and enduring. Every online action, from the websites visited to the emails sent, is logged and stored away in an NSA database, able to be retrieved at any time. This creates a detailed and potentially incriminating record that can be used by governments not just to track criminal activity but also to monitor political dissent and control populations.

Hoover's reign at the FBI was marred with multiple controversies, COINTELPRO included. Short for Counter Intelligence Program, it was a covert effort created in 1956 to "expose, disrupt, misdirect, discredit, or otherwise neutralize" the activities of individuals and organizations the FBI considered subversive. These efforts were focused on various political organizations and leaders, including Martin Luther King, Jr. FBI officials sent King an anonymous letter, known now as the "suicide letter," suggesting he kill himself. They bugged his hotel rooms, hoping to uncover salacious details to ruin his reputation. And it wasn't just King. His family, friends, and associates were all subject to this unwarranted and insidious invasion of privacy. COINTELPRO also aimed its shadowy operations at the Southern Christian Leadership Conference, the Student Nonviolent Coordinating Committee, the Black Panther Party, and anti-Vietnam War activists. Even harmless groups promoting racial and gender equality found themselves on the FBI's hit list.

Successful as they were, Hoover and his team were stuck in an analog world, limited by the technology of the team. Today is a new day, and the NSA experiences no such restrictions. With a click of a button, government agents can gain access to a massive data dump on any individual, whether they're suspected of a crime or not. This permanent record of each individual sits in a database, with new information being added in real time, accessible to anyone with the right security clearance. Over the decades, the NSA's access to information and power to utilize it has grown, evolving with various Congressional authorizations. None, however, can compare to the USA PATRIOT Act.

Known officially as the "Uniting and Strengthening America by Providing Appropriate Tools Required to Intercept and Obstruct Terrorism Act of 2001," or unofficially as the "Patriot Act," it was passed just a few weeks after the 9/11 attacks after a supermajority of congressmen. This law greatly expanded the surveillance capabilities of the United States government. Initially presented as a necessary tool to combat terrorism, it also allowed unprecedented access to personal information. The PATRIOT Act facilitated the collection of vast amounts of data, including phone records, internet activity, and financial transactions—enabling the NSA to set up the systems that Snowden later exposed. This legislation effectively turned the tools of surveillance inward, targeting not only potential terrorists but also the general populace. The broad and vague definitions of "terrorism" and "national security threats" enabled the NSA and other agencies to cast a wide net, ensnaring ordinary citizens in their data-gathering operations.

The NSA's digital surveillance capabilities have set the stage for an unprecedented reduction in privacy and freedom. By leveraging advanced technology, the government can now maintain a detailed and permanent record of every individual's digital activities—as well as their physical activities—by tracking their location and proximity to other people. This shift has empowered the state to monitor and control populations with ease, such as China's "social credit score" system, turning surveillance tools inward and undermining the fundamental principles of privacy and liberty. The broad reach of these capabilities, justified under the guise of national security, threatens to create a society where personal freedom is a relic of the past.

Why is it the Worst Idea?

In 2005, a military officer was granted access to the NSA's surveillance data, and on the first day on the job, he entered the email addresses of six of his ex-girlfriends to see what information he could find on them. The year before, an NSA spy snooped on calls of a number she had found in her husband's cell phone records because she suspected he had been unfaithful. In 2011, an NSA employee spied on the calls of her boyfriend and others she had recently met. Over and over again, people with access to these systems have accessed them for personal reasons. No one who has been caught has been fired, nor has anyone been arrested or prosecuted.

Yet NSA Chief Keith Alexander claimed publicly that "no one has willfully or knowingly disobeyed the law or tried to invade your civil liberties or privacy." It was a completely false statement, just as it was when James Clapper, Director of National Intelligence, testified before Congress on March 15, 2013. "Does the NSA collect any type of data at all on millions or hundreds of millions of Americans?" Senator Ron Wyden asked Clapper. "No, sir," Clapper replied. Again, it was a lie—and this lie, in particular, is what motivated Snowden to blow the lid open on the whole operation.

The NSA intercepts nearly two billion communications every day, amassing a gargantuan database filled with your data. It does not delete this information; it grows over time, learning more and more about you—and empowering anyone with access to learn all kinds of things about you. But by no means is it the sole surveillance system in existence; other federal agencies, as well as state and local governments, all maintain databases with significant personal information—tracking people's location, biometric information (fingerprints, DNA, facial recognition data, etc.), financial data, and much more. These systems, combined with the NSA's capabilities, form a sprawling surveillance network that can piece together a comprehensive picture of individuals' lives, often without their knowledge or consent. And these systems are similarly abused; an Associated Press investigation in 2016 found hundreds of examples of law enforcement officers inappropriately accessing and using collected data on citizens.

Alexis Delany is one of countless victims of the government's creation and use of the "Permanent Record"—a long history of data compiled about each person. Her ex-boyfriend was a police officer and accessed her information to stalk her. "It's personal. It's your address. It's all your information, it's your Social Security number, it's everything about you," Delany said. "And when they use it for ill purposes to commit crimes against you—to stalk you, to follow you, to harass you… it just becomes so dangerous." She's not wrong. The pervasive reach of these surveillance systems creates an environment where personal data is constantly at risk of being misused. The sheer volume of data collected creates a huge temptation for abuse.

The cases of government employees misusing their access for personal reasons are not anomalies; they highlight how this system is rotten at its core. When individuals can tap into vast amounts of private data without meaningful oversight or consequences, the potential for abuse skyrockets—and as evidenced by their leaders lying to Congress and the public, these government agencies are extremely untrustworthy and the last institutions on Earth that should be in control of such sensitive and significant data.

The very existence of a massive government-owned database containing intimate details about people's lives threatens the principles of a free society—the right of assembly, the right to seek redress of your grievances, the right to privacy, and so on. If Big Brother is cataloging your every move, that creates a chilling effect whereby people self-censor, self-limit, and do not speak out for fear of being tracked, caught, and punished. This is why communist countries like China love surveillance systems, for they can wield totalitarian power over people's lives by monitoring their movements, their actions, their online activity, and more. A permanent record of each person is the dream of dystopian dictators and has no place in "the land of the free."

It's one thing to actively surveil people—to access information on a phone call they're making or where they are located. But the government's database archives *historical* information—all your past emails and phone calls and texts and DMs and photos and financial information and location information and much more. By knowing you deeply—your past behaviors and communications—those in power can more easily predict (and control) your future actions. It's not just about what you're doing now; it's about everything you've ever done—meticulously recorded and forever accessible. In a permanent record, nothing is private. Put simply, the dream of freedom cannot coexist with the nightmare of a surveillance state.

A World Without It

Consider the worst thing you've ever done—your most shameful secret. Imagine that this embarrassing event has somehow found its way online. When future romantic partners, employers, or even your grandchildren search your name, that incident could be easily uncovered. In our interconnected world, a reputation can be destroyed in minutes, leaving a person perpetually defined by their past mistake. This discovery could cause significant personal harm, and the fear of such exposure might lead you to alter your behavior both online and offline to avoid the risk of unwanted attention or having to deal with the judgment of others. Now, think of the most unpleasant person you've ever encountered—perhaps a bully you've had dealings with before. Now consider this person being empowered to access your secret—and the secrets of anyone he wants to target.

It sounds horrifying—the easy access to people's personal details, exploited by awful people. The sheer amount of digital data generated about each of us—our calendar events, our photos, our conversations, our financial data, our health data, and much more—means that as these databases grow and as our digital footprint expands, we become tethered to all our past actions, making it near impossible to escape them.

This is why some privacy advocates have pursued legal reforms centered around a concept called "the right to be forgotten." This principle allows individuals to request (or demand) the removal of personal information from Internet companies, particularly information that is no longer relevant or that could harm their reputation. It aims to give people control over their digital footprint, enabling them to move past their mistakes and start anew. The goal is to protect individuals from the perpetual shadow of their past and ensure that their privacy is respected in the digital age.

As nice as it may be to expunge from the Internet details about your past that you want hidden, that data will still reside, as part of your permanent record, in a government database—ready for retrieval by anyone with the right security clearance. Even if public-facing information can be scrubbed, the data stored in government databases remains intact, subject to access and potential misuse by those in power. And why? For what purposes? Proponents of these systems argue that they are essential in order to combat terrorism and protect national security—that the more information they have at their disposal, the better they can fight crime and preserve the peace.

Not quite. This argument is no different than saying a totalitarian government is helpful in maintaining security and peace—for if the government can control people's every action, then it can ensure that those actions do not cause problems for anyone (including the government). In reality, people are not more secure, but their basic freedoms have been violated. So, too, with the surveillance state; it hasn't stopped terrorism or protected national security, but it has, in fact, radically expanded the power of the government to violate people's right to privacy.

So what would society look like if it were free from the gaze of Big Brother? Yes, there would still be crime—but instead of violating the rights of countless innocent people in the hopes of catching a bad guy, law enforcement would have to focus their investigation solely on suspects. No longer would government officials be able to go on "fishing expeditions," searching through large databases with all our information, in order to get the data they needed. Our information, as innocent citizens, would be ours to control and keep private. The permanent record would be deleted, and with it, the ability of those in power to use and abuse our data.

Months before Snowden revealed to the world what the government was up to—and the staggering amount of data it was compiling about all of us—the Chief Technology Officer for the CIA, Ira Hunt, gave a speech at a tech conference in New York. In it, he warned that the government was trying to collect all information and keep it forever. "The value of any piece of information is only known," he said, "when you can connect it with something else that arrives at a future point in time. Since you can't connect dots you don't have… we fundamentally try to collect everything and hang on to it forever." Essentially, the government doesn't know who will be a criminal in the future, so in the off chance you might turn into one, they would want at that future date to be able to look up your entire history and know precisely who you are, what you've done, where you've been, and with whom you've communicated. "It is nearly within our grasp," Hunt said, "to compute on all human generated information."

It doesn't have to be this way. Shutting down these surveillance systems would allow individuals the freedom to live without the perpetual shadow of their past actions, both good and bad. Crime would still be solved. And there would be more peace—and, importantly, less potential for the government to abuse its own citizens. At its core, this concept is incompatible with a free society. Permanent records are dystopian tools to centralize power and control others. Aspiring instead for a utopian future requires us to abolish them.

Tuttle Twins Takeaways

1. A digital world expands the surveillance capabilities of the government, allowing it to collect comprehensive data on each citizen.

2. This information becomes archived permanently, for later retrieval, creating a permanent record of past activities, communications, whereabouts, and more.

3. Maintaining databases like this empowers the government to violate people's rights easily and without their knowledge.

4. Surveilling people creates a chilling effect where people self-censor and alter their actions due to the fear of being monitored and punished.

5. Mass surveillance undermines the principles of a free society by enabling constant monitoring of innocent people.

BUREAUCRACY

Inefficient and corrupt administrative
systems contributed to the collapse of
powerful empires throughout history—
and history is repeating itself today.

"Behind the ostensible
government sits enthroned an
invisible government owing no
allegiance and acknowledging
no responsibility to the people."

~ Teddy Roosevelt

Why did the powerful Roman Empire collapse? There are, of course, numerous reasons: a distracted and debauched citizenry; a devalued currency impoverishing everyone except the elite; or relentless invasions by barbarian tribes. But there is another answer, and it's one that is often overlooked. The clue is contained in a book called *The Decline and Fall of the Roman Empire*, written by Edward Gibbon in the late eighteenth century. In his book, Gibbon observed a shift in governance between the early Empire and its later stages:

> "The number of ministers, of magistrates, of officers, and of servants, who filled the different departments of the state, was multiplied beyond the example of former times; and… when the proportion of those who received exceeded the proportion of those who contributed the provinces were oppressed by the weight of tributes. From this period to the extinction of the empire it would be easy to deduce an uninterrupted series of clamors and complaints.

In layman's terms, Rome fell in large part due to the largess of the government; the Empire's sophisticated system of administration to govern its vast territories—with thousands of provincial governors, military officials, tax collectors, and civil officers—became too much to bear. It was what we now call bureaucracy: the administration of a government by unelected, full-time individuals organized into various departments and offices, each with a sphere of responsibility and authority to oversee and control the actions of those in their domain.

This elaborate system, initially designed to maintain order and efficiency, gradually turned into a cumbersome behemoth. The sheer number of officials and the overlapping layers of authority led to inefficiencies, rampant corruption, and a disconnect between the central government and the local administrations. There were too many unproductive mouths that needed to be fed, supplied by the heavily taxed productive class who had to take care of an increasingly large number of government workers. The bureaucratic machine, instead of facilitating governance, began to suffocate the empire, contributing to its eventual downfall.

This pattern of bureaucratic overreach and inefficiency is certainly not unique to ancient Rome; many other governments have discovered the necessity of subdividing authority among thousands of bureaucrats in order to manage a growing government. Consider the case of the Union of Soviet Socialist Republics (USSR), a communist country that spanned much of Eurasia for nearly seven decades. Driven by their socialist ideology, those in power—who had overthrown their predecessors in a military coup—wielded that power to control others' lives in pursuit of Marx's idea of utopia. That meant centralizing decision-making authority instead of letting people freely choose their preferred outcomes in pursuit of their individual desires.

In the USSR, the government centralized decision-making for many aspects of life that individuals would normally handle themselves. For example, the state controlled agricultural production through collective farms, eliminating farmers' ability to make decisions about their own land. Housing was also state-managed, with people assigned apartments by the government rather than choosing where to live. Consumer goods were distributed through state-run stores with a limited selection, restricting personal choice in purchases. Education and career paths were centrally planned, often determining individuals' futures based on government needs rather than personal interests. Additionally, travel within and outside the country was heavily regulated, requiring government permission and limiting personal freedom of movement.

Managing the affairs of millions of people is no easy task. So the Soviets created departments and government bureaus for nearly everything—a massive bureaucracy that became notorious for its inefficiency, corruption, and rigidity. They had the Ministry of Heavy Industry, the Ministry of Agriculture, the Ministry of Transport, the Ministry of Culture, and many more. Layers upon layers of officials and committees were created to oversee every aspect of life. Decisions were made by a small elite at the top and then passed down through the ranks. This top-down approach led to a lack of responsiveness and adaptability, as local officials were often unable or unwilling to deviate from prescribed plans, even when faced with on-the-ground realities that required different solutions. Corruption was rampant, as bureaucrats exploited their positions for personal gain, further undermining the effectiveness of the government. It was, as you might imagine, a nightmare.

You might also imagine that, seeing its failures in Rome and the USSR, the United States of America would steer clear of bureaucracy in order to avoid rotting from within, as happened in both of these empires. You would be wrong.

The Context

After its creation, the newly constituted United States government was small; the original bureaucracy, if you can even call it that, consisted only of employees from three small departments—State, Treasury, and War. Washington's cabinet—a fraction of the size of today's presidential cabinets—thus only included secretaries in charge of each department as well as the Attorney General. The simplicity and modest size of this early bureaucracy reflected the limited scope of federal responsibilities in the country's early years. The Constitution had empowered this government only with limited powers, and that meant not many people were required.

As the country enlarged its borders westward, the size of government grew—and with it, the people on payroll to administer its functions. New agencies were created to manage the land and its settlement—for example, the General Land Office in 1812 and the Department of the Interior in 1849. This era marked the beginning of a more complex and expansive federal bureaucracy. And when war broke out between the states, the number of government jobs surged to handle the demands of warfare. The need to mobilize and supply a large military, manage wartime logistics, and address the aftermath of the conflict required significant administrative capacity.

By far, the largest growth of the bureaucracy in American history came between 1933 and 1945. Franklin D. Roosevelt's "New Deal" meant bigger government, since numerous agencies were needed to administer his many programs. Agencies like the Works Progress Administration, the Social Security Administration, and the Civilian Conservation Corps were created in response to the Great Depression. And with the American entry into World War II in 1941, the number of federal agencies and employees skyrocketed further—with agencies like the Office of War

Mobilization, the War Production Board, and many others. During FDR's twelve years in office, the total number of federal employees increased from a little over half a million in 1933 to an all-time high of more than 3.5 million in 1945.

Amid this bureaucratic surge and in a moment of self-reflection, the newly organized President's Committee on Administrative Management surveyed the landscape of federal workers in the executive branch in hopes of identifying ways to make the administration of government more efficient and effective. Their conclusion?

> Without plan or intent, there has grown up a headless "fourth branch" of the government, responsible to no one, and impossible of coordination with the general policies and work of the government as determined by the people through their duly elected representatives.

This result—called either the "administrative state" or the "deep state"—refers to the vast network of unelected officials, agencies, and bureaucratic institutions that operate with considerable autonomy and influence, often beyond the direct control of elected representatives who are typically unaware of their existence or activities. As the federal government expanded, so, too, did the power and reach of this administrative apparatus, which began to function as a separate entity within the government. The "fourth branch" of government, as it was dubbed, grew in size and complexity; as the Committee noted, it had "been clearly recognized for a generations and has been growing steadily worse decade by decade."

These agencies have built up an arsenal of administrative law—effectively, rules that are written separate from the laws passed by Congress—which people are obligated to obey. Beyond merely creating these new rules, which have the force of law, the agencies themselves enforce them—acting as prosecutor, judge, and jury. This concentration of power within the administrative state is a significant departure from the system of checks and balances envisioned by the Founders, where legislative, executive, and judicial powers were meant to be distinct and balanced against each other. It gives agencies unchecked discretion to wield power that violates individual liberty, property rights, and due process. To give an example, in a single recent year, Congress enacted 138 laws while federal agencies created 2,926 new administrative rules. And while federal judges held around 95,000 trials, the agencies conducted nearly one million. Put simply, the executive branch has been claiming the powers of the other two branches of government. So much for checks and balances.

Nearly three million people work for the federal government today; Washington's tiny cabinet has grown far, far larger. Today, bureaucrats work for a wide variety of government groups: The Committee for the Implementation of Textile Agreements; The Office of Financial Education; The National Potato Promotion Board; The National Helium Reserve; The Federal Interagency Committee for the Management of Noxious and Exotic Weeds; The National Center for Complementary and Integrative Health; The National Honey Board; The Office of Pesticide Programs; and countless others. These agencies and offices, often dedicated to niche concerns and highly specialized areas, reflect the sprawling reach of federal power into nearly every aspect of American life. They demonstrate in vivid terms how the federal government's bureaucracy has expanded far beyond its original scope.

In recent decades, their power—the administrative state's influence on people's everyday lives—grew because of a 1984 US Supreme Court case, *Chevron U.S.A., Inc. v. Natural Resources Defense Council, Inc.* This ruling established the precedent that courts should defer to federal agencies' interpretations of ambiguous laws—a decision that significantly empowered the administrative state by allowing unelected bureaucrats to effectively create and enforce laws without direct accountability. This, of course, reinforced the dangers of an unchecked bureaucracy that operates with minimal oversight from the judiciary or Congress. The Court effectively blessed the activities of the administrative state and severed any significant accountability that might check its growth. It created a disaster.

Why is it the Worst Idea?

Loper Bright Enterprises is a family-owned fishing company based in New Jersey. Like other fishing companies, they were required to spend around $700 every day to pay federal bureaucrats who would board their vessels to monitor their fishing activities. These monitors, employed by the National Marine Fisheries Service (NMFS), were tasked with ensuring compliance with federal regulations—regulations that govern everything from the type of fish caught to the methods used. For many small fishing companies, this extra financial burden can make the difference between staying afloat or being forced out of business.

Congress never authorized the NMFS to compel fishing companies to pay up like this, so Loper Bright sued. It was an uphill battle because of the *Chevron* case; if the US

Supreme Court had already empowered federal agencies to reasonably regulate even without Congressional authorization, what hope could a few fishermen have? The answer is little to none if you consider Loper Bright's legal fight. In February 2020, Loper filed a lawsuit in the United States District Court for the District of Columbia, alleging that Congress had not authorized the NMFS to mandate industry-funded monitoring of herring fisheries. The court ruled in favor of the agency, citing the *Chevron* case. Loper Bright appealed to the United States Court of Appeals, which sided with the District Court. To their credit, Loper Bright and their legal team soldiered on, soliciting the US Supreme Court to take up the case. The Court agreed, heard the case, and on June 28, 2024, issued their ruling striking down *Chevron* deference.

While many champions of limited government were rightly thrilled with the overturning of decades of bureaucratic empowerment, we should have low expectations for how much the administrative state will shrink. After all, as Thomas Jefferson said, "The natural progress of things is for liberty to yield, and government to gain ground." Anyone who has acquired power—from busybody bureaucrats to demagogue dictators—desires to defend and increase that power from any and all threats. Bureaucracy is like cancer, resisting efforts to contain it and constantly seeking to expand its reach. The entrenched nature of the administrative state, with its vast network of agencies, regulations, and unelected officials, makes it a formidable force that will not easily be dismantled. These bureaucratic entities have become deeply embedded in the fabric of government, growing long before *Chevron* came around in 1984. One court ruling will not dismantle the deep state.

But bureaucracy, for all its many faults, is merely a symptom of something else far more dangerous: the centralization of power. Think of Washington's administration, small in size and power. Most political power was decentralized—meaning that it was diffused among state and local governments, if at all. Often, power was retained by the people themselves. Thus, the 10th Amendment to the US Constitution (though widely ignored by today's government) states that powers not expressly granted by the Constitution "are reserved to the States respectively, or to the people." Power was localized, and by doing that, there was no need for a gargantuan government at the federal level. But time went on, and circumstances presented opportunities for those in power to take even more of it. Wars, economic crises, public health threats, political rivalries, population increase, and many more factors enabled power-hungry politicians to justify new laws, new departments, new agencies, and more government.

Centralizing power concentrates decision-making authority in the hands of a few, reducing accountability and radically increasing the potential for abuse. When power is centralized, it becomes easier for those in control to impose their will on the entire population, often without adequate checks and balances. As James Madison wrote in *Federalist* No. 47, "The accumulation of all powers, legislative, executive, and judiciary, in the same hands, whether of one, a few, or many… may justly be pronounced the very definition of tyranny." Bureaucracy and its cause— the concentration of government power—are therefore a threat to liberty. People cannot be free if their actions are micromanaged by those who are paid to meddle in people's private affairs. By limiting people's actions with endless rules, bureaucracy discourages innovation, inhibits risk-taking, and crushes creativity. It is a tax on human achievement—and one that has far too high a cost.

A World Without It

Like many others in her position, Tara was completely caught off guard when she was diagnosed with cancer. She was, by all measures, a healthy and active twenty-eight-year-old bride-to-be living her best life in Pennsylvania. But an unusual lump in her neck gave her cause for concern, which she initially dismissed until she couldn't any longer. A biopsy confirmed she had Hodgkin lymphoma, a cancer originating from white blood cells. A whirlwind of emotions engulfed her in the days following, but the path before her was clear: she would fight the cancer with chemotherapy. Patients in her position all come to realize that these invasive cells will continue to grow throughout their body unless checked; it is in their nature to replicate and take over other cells. There is no way out but through a frontal assault. Cancer can't be persuaded to stop; it must be beaten.

This presents a pattern for how bureaucracy will end; Jefferson's observation about the natural growth of government was spot on. Centralized power won't surrender with persuasive words; those who enjoy control won't relinquish it easily. This suggests that tweaking laws here and there, or even a US Supreme Court case, will be inadequate to eliminate the problem. Like Henry David Thoreau said, "There are a thousand hacking at the branches of evil to one who is striking at the root." If we want a world without bureaucracy and its ridiculous micromanagement of individuals, then we have to strike at its root: the centralization of political power. We must decentralize power as the Founders did. Easier said than done, right?

Karl Marx once wrote, "Bureaucracy is a circle no one can leave." He was wrong. This condition of regulating human activity is not a given; there are no laws of nature that say we must submit to this situation. Imagine for a moment if we were successful in our goal of centralizing power—of tearing down the size and scope of the state to resemble what Washington's cabinet first looked like. What might that outcome look like—a world where the circle simply does not exist?

For starters, fishermen wouldn't have to pay people to watch them fish. People wouldn't need a permit to paint their fence their desired color. Kids could sell lemonade on their driveway without needing a food handler's permit. Farmers wouldn't be required to complete environmental impact assessments before planting crops or installing new irrigation systems. Residents wouldn't need permission to cut down trees on their own property. Parents wouldn't have to get approval to educate their own children. Protestors wouldn't be confined to "free speech zones." People could own pets without a license. Farmers wouldn't be fined for selling raw milk. Developers could build without having to navigate an endless maze of permits and fees.

This sounds like freedom to many—and it is—but to others, it sounds downright scary. Jefferson referred to these cowards who find comfort in government control, saying they prefer "the calm of despotism to the tempestuous sea of liberty." Bureaucracy creates calm—predictability, stability, and regulated behavior. You can wrap your head around it. There are documented processes, hoops to jump through, and multiple layers of oversight to limit anything that could be disruptive or unpredictable. Many people embrace that calm, even if it is, as Madison noted, "the very definition of tyranny." If you were to propose abolishing The Federal Interagency Committee for the Management of Noxious and Exotic Weeds or The Committee for the Implementation of Textile Agreements, these people would ask: what would you replace them with? "When you remove a cancer," asked economist Thomas Sowell in retort, "what do you replace it with?" The obvious answer is nothing.

This vision of freedom may seem radical, even frightening, to those who have grown accustomed to the predictability of bureaucracy. But true liberty is not found in the calm waters of bureaucratic control—it is found in the vibrant, sometimes chaotic, but ultimately empowering sea of individual freedom and personal responsibility. A world without unnecessary regulations, permits, and bureaucratic red tape—a world without a "fourth branch" of government comprised of micromanagers and busybodies—is one where innovation, prosperity, and freedom can flourish. It is a world where individuals are trusted to make their own decisions and where communities are free to govern themselves. It is a world, put simply, where freedom is not just an ideal or aspiration, but a lived reality.

Tuttle Twins Takeaways

1. Bureaucracy played a significant role in the downfall of past empires and nation-states by creating inefficiency, corruption, and unmanageable administrative systems.

2. The growth of bureaucracy in the United States, particularly during and after the New Deal, has expanded federal power far beyond its original constitutional limits.

3. The administrative state represents a vast, unaccountable network of unelected officials who wield significant influence over the lives of citizens.

4. Centralized power is dangerous because it concentrates decision-making authority in the hands of a few, increasing the potential for tyranny and reducing individual freedom.

5. Bureaucracy stifles innovation, creativity, and personal responsibility by imposing unnecessary regulations and micromanaging individuals' lives.

Phew! There are clearly a lot of bad ideas out there. Knowing more about them can help us recognize and fight them in order to spread *good* and *true* ideas instead.

After all, that's what the world really is—a clash of ideas between different people, many of whom are trying to gain political power so they can *impose* their ideas on everyone else. The more we can see these flawed ideas, the better we'll be able to slow or stop their spread.

Ideas have power. They lead to action, change culture, and alter our perception of ourselves and the world around us. If we're armed with powerful, true ideas—and better yet, if we know how to persuade others to believe these ideas as well—then we'll be very effective in the war of ideas.

Why a war? Because ideas can kill! Whether it's gun control laws that disarm victims, Marxist economic failures that starve many to death, or neoconservative foreign policies that kill innocent people in faraway lands, dangerous ideas can be—and are—destructive.

That's why we have to win the war. We need to understand the truth. We need to learn about—and learn how to defend—good ideas. We need to make these ideas popular.

And you can help! No matter your age, you can be someone who shares good ideas with others. (And who, when necessary, points out bad ideas too!)

How can you do this?

It's as easy as sharing one of our books with a friend. Or you can start a book club. Maybe write a letter to the editor of your local newspaper or start your own blog.

With a parent's permission, you could even start a podcast. Or if you're really ambitious, write a book of your own!

Whatever you choose, we need you in the fight. Good ideas that aren't defended will languish. These ideas need us to stand up and fight error with truth.

See you on the battlefield!

—The Tuttle Twins